# LANGUAGE AND LITERACY SERIES

Dorothy S. Strickland, FOUNDING EDITOR

Celia Genishi and Donna E. Alvermann, SERIES EDITORS

ADVISORY BOARD: Richard Allington, Kathryn Au, Bernice Cullinan, Colette Daiute, Anne Haas Dyson,
Carole Edelsky, Shirley Brice Heath, Connie Juel, Susan Lytle, Timothy Shanahan

(continued)

or volumes in the NCRLL Collection (edited by JoBeth Allen and Donna E. Alvermann) and the Practitioners Bookshelf Series (edited by
elia Genishi and Donna E. Alvermann), as well as a complete list of titles in this series, please visit www.tcpress.com.

# Inspiring Dialogue

## TALKING TO LEARN IN THE ENGLISH CLASSROOM

*Mary M. Juzwik*
*Carlin Borsheim-Black*
*Samantha Caughlan*
*Anne Heintz*

Foreword by
Martin Nystrand

TEACHERS COLLEGE PRESS

TEACHERS COLLEGE | COLUMBIA UNIVERSITY
NEW YORK AND LONDON

Published by Teachers College Press, 1234 Amsterdam Avenue, New York, NY 10027

*Library of Congress Cataloging-in-Publication Data*

Juzwik, Mary M. (Mary Margaret)
    Inspiring dialogue : talking to learn in the English classroom / Mary M. Juzwik,
  Carlin Borsheim-Black, Samantha Caughlan, Anne Heintz ; foreword by
  Martin Nystrand.
        pages cm. — (Language and literacy series)
    Includes bibliographical references and index.
    ISBN 978-0-8077-5467-2 (pbk. : alk. paper)
    ISBN 978-0-8077-5468-9 (hardcover : alk. paper)
    1. Dialogic teaching. 2. English language—Study and teaching (Elementary)
  3. English language—Study and teaching (Secondary) I. Title.
    LB1029.D48J89 2013
    371.102—dc23                                                    2013018918

ISBN 978-0-8077-5467-2 (paperback)
ISBN 978-0-8077-5468-9 (hardcover)
eISBN 978-0-8077-7263-8 (eBook)

Printed on acid-free paper
Manufactured in the United States of America

20  19  18  17  16                    8  7  6  5  4  3  2

*For Joanna Juzwik McDonald,*
*Joshua Juzwik, and Sarah Glenn,*
*lifelong conversational partners*
*—MJ*

*For my first teachers,*
*Eugene and Christeen Borsheim*
*—CB*

*To Steven Brown,*
*in celebration of thirty years of dialogue*
*—SC*

*For my parents*
*—AH*

# Contents

# Foreword

In 1966, an important professional conference that has come to be known as the Dartmouth Seminar convened mainly American and British researchers in English, linguistics, education, and psychology to survey and make recommendations for improving elementary and secondary English instruction. In his report of the proceedings, *Growth through English*, John Dixon (1967) emphasized personal growth as the focus of the field's reform mission, in contrast to traditional emphases on cultural heritage and skills. This emphasis highlighted the work of several British Dartmouth Seminar participants, including James Britton, Douglas Barnes, and Harold Rosen. Britton in particular distinguished the important learning role of exploratory and expressive talk and writing in which the demands of correctness were relaxed and teacher judgments were suspended to allow and encourage students to develop sustained trains of thought. Britton's "Talking to Learn" (1969) and "Writing to Learn and Learning to Write" (1972) captured the new epistemologies and emphases for English.

Until recently, however, Britton's advocation for talking to learn failed to cross the Atlantic as classroom discourse continued apace to be dominated by lecture and recitation. It was not until 1991 that Adam Gamoran and I published the first-time-ever results of a large-scale empirical study (Nystrand & Gamoran, 1991) finding positive student achievement effects in middle and high school English and reading instruction for open-ended discussion and such dialogic moves as authentic teacher questions and uptake (first studied by Collins, 1982), both regarded as aspects of teacher-student interaction foregrounding the importance of student engagement and thinking.

This research could not have been done without the Western introduction of Russian philosopher and literary theorist Mikhail Bakhtin in the mid-1970s. Together with a few colleagues known as the Bakhtin Circle, Bakhtin articulated how dialogue shapes both language and thought. The perspective inspired by him has come to be called *dialogism*. Utterances were interesting to Bakhtin because he saw that they respond to previous utterances at the same time that they anticipate future responses. In this view, discourse is continuously woven into a "chain of speech communication" by one speaker's "responsive position" relative to another. Discourse is dialogic not because the speakers take turns but rather because it is continually structured by tension—indeed even conflict—between the conversants, between self and other as one voice "refracts" the other. It is precisely this tension—this relationship between self and other, this juxtaposition of relative perspectives and struggle among competing voices—that for Bakhtin gives shape to all discourse and hence lies at the heart of understanding as a dynamic, sociocognitive event.

In *Inspiring Dialogue*, Mary Juzwik, Carlin Borsheim-Black, Samantha Caughlan, and Anne Heintz document just how well established this conception of instruction and classroom discourse has become in both the United States and Europe. Since our initial empirical work was published in the early 1990s, dialogically organized instruction has been shown in numerous large-scale studies to correlate with student achievement in reading and literature (e.g., Applebee, Langer, Nystrand, & Gamoran, 2003; Langer, 2001; Murphy, Wilkinson, Soter, Hennessey, & Alexander, 2009; Nystrand, 1997).

*Inspiring Dialogue* is, moreover, a practical handbook for student teachers, professional development personnel, and practicing teachers aiming to open up their instruction to fuller student engagement and more discriminating writing. *Inspiring Dialogue* covers a comprehensive and practical set of tools and strategies for implementing dialogic instruction. It grapples with current challenges such as prescribed curricula, standardized testing, and standards-based instruction. It notes the importance of dialogic instruction to civic discourse that is too often challenged in today's polarized politics. And it is a program that has been fully tested at Michigan State University in one of the most thorough and carefully crafted teacher education programs nationally. Unique for a handbook for teaching, their recommendations are completely supported by a careful empirical study of the effectiveness of their program preparing new teachers to design dialogically organized classroom environments (Caughlan, Juzwik, Borsheim-Black, Kelly, & Fine, 2013).

—Martin Nystrand

## REFERENCES

Applebee, A., Langer, J., Nystrand, M., & Gamoran, A. (2003). Discussion-based approaches to developing understanding: Classroom instruction and student performance in middle and high school English. *American Educational Research Journal, 40*(3), 685–730.

Britton, J. (1969) Talking to learn. In D. Barnes, J. Britton, & H. Rosen (Eds.), *Language, the learner and the school* (pp. 79–115). Harmondsworth, UK: Penguin.

Britton, J. (1972). Writing to learn and learning to write. In National Council of Teachers of English (Ed.), *The humanity of English: NCTE distinguished lectures* (pp. 32–53). Urbana, IL: National Council of Teachers of English.

Caughlan, S., Juzwik, M., Borsheim-Black, C., Kelly, S., & Fine, J. (2013). *Research in the Teaching of English, 47*(3), 212–246.

Collins, J. (1982). Discourse style, classroom interaction, and differential treatment. *Journal of Reading Behavior, 14,* 429–437.

Dixon, J. (1967). *Growth through English.* London: Cox & Wyman.

Langer, J. A. (2001). Beating the odds: Teaching middle and high school students to read and write well. *American Educational Research Journal, 38*(4), 837–880.

Murphy, P. K., Wilkinson, I. A. G., Soter, A. O., Hennessey, M. N., & Alexander, J. F. (2009). Examining the effects of classroom discussion on students' high-level comprehension of text: A meta-analysis. *Journal of Educational Psychology, 101,* 740–764.

Nystrand, M. (with Gamoran, A., Kachur, R., & Prendergast, C.). (1997). *Opening dialogue: Understanding the dynamics of language and learning in the English classroom.* New York: Teachers College Press.

Nystrand, M., & Gamoran, A. (1991). Instructional discourse, student engagement, and literature achievement. *Research in the Teaching of English, 25,* 261–290.

# Acknowledgments

This book is truly the result of a series of dialogic collaborations. We thank two cohorts of new teachers from the English education program featured in this book, who agreed to participate in our research project and to share their hard work with us and with each other. We have been inspired by their openness to engaging new practices and technologies while learning to teach. We also thank the experienced teachers whose examples we refer to in the book, Lucia Elden and Rae Belmont, for opening their classroom doors to us.

Conversations with colleagues in the College of Education at Michigan State University have pushed our thinking about teacher preparation and student learning throughout the project: Alicia Alonzo, Dorothea Anagnostopoulos, Angela Calabrese-Barton, Janine Certo, Nell Duke, Lynn Fendler, Matt Ferkany, Susan Florio-Ruane, Kyle Greenwalt, Beth Herbel-Eisenmann, George Harnick, Mary Lundeberg, Gail Richmond, Cheryl Rosaen, Christina Schwarz, Avner Segall, Michael Steele, Gary Sykes, Trudy Sykes, Tanya Wright, and Peter Youngs. Suzanne Wilson's stalwart leadership facilitated the intellectual, pedagogical, and logistical work of the project. We are also grateful to colleagues "across the river" who have sharpened our writing: Ellen Cushman, Nancy DeJoy, Julie Lindquist, Leonora Smith, and Marilyn Wilson. Thanks to Terri Gustafson and Scott Schopieray for their technical support.

We also thank our colleagues in the field who have discussed dialogic teaching and related problems with us over the years: Mary Adler, Arthur Applebee, Richard Beach, Maureen Boyd, Jory Brass, Anne Haas Dyson, Adam Gamoran, James Gee, Amanda Godley, Nelson Graff, George Hillocks, Eileen Kaiser, Sean Kelly, Judith Langer, Martin Nystrand, Robert Petrone, Eija Rougle, Peter Smagorinsky, Amanda Haertling Thein, Ian Wilkinson, and Stanton Wortham.

Thank you to colleagues who generously offered thoughtful feedback on full drafts of the book manuscript: Christine Dawson, Amy Carpenter Ford, David Adams, Miriam Frieden, and Kathy Morcom. We greatly benefited from feedback and input on sections of the developing manuscript from April Baker-Bell, Jeff Bale, Julie Bell, Sakeena Everett, Jihea Kang, Kati Macaluso, Mike Macaluso, Cori McKenzie, Django Paris, Natasha Perez, Doug Shraufnagle, Erik Skogsberg,

Amanda Smith, and Jon Wargo. Michael B. Sherry and Kelly Z. Merritt helped shape early pedagogical work on the project. We greatly appreciate Jaymee Mason's willingness to assist us in coding hundreds of classroom transcripts.

We are grateful to editor Emily Spangler for seeing the possibilities for a new book on classroom talk and for offering enthusiastic support and spot-on critical feedback throughout the manuscript development process. We also thank Aureliano Vazquez Jr. for keeping the project on schedule throughout the production process.

We thank our own teaching mentors who have inspired us to open dialogues with students: Jeanne Heintz, Susie Heintz, Kerry Demers, Louis Gallien, Linda Adler-Kassner, Larry and Trish Shumate, and Jim Keeney.

Thanks to Joe Byers and Lucy Bates-Byers for supporting our teacher education development work through the Bates-Byers Award for Curriculum and Technology. The Spencer Foundation Small Grants Program supported the research grounding the claims about dialogic tools throughout the book.

Finally, we owe a deep debt of gratitude to our families, who see a little less of us each time we get ourselves involved in another project. Our heartfelt thanks to Matt and Maudemarie, Stuart and Marcus, Steven, and Jim, Jack, and Alex.

# PART I

# A Dialogic Stance

Part 1 orients you to the overarching theme of the book—cultivating a dialogic stance to inspire learning talk in your classroom. More specifically, Chapter 1 introduces you to our idea of dialogic teaching: It is not just about discussion-based teaching, although discussions are important, but about developing a repertoire of classroom talk practices to support your teaching goals. Taking such a stance means that any instructional designs and practices providing students with frequent and sustained opportunities to engage in learning talk count as dialogic teaching. Chapter 1 also makes the case for why dialogic teaching is needed now more than ever before: Not only does it support students' literacy achievement learning and classroom engagement, but it also prepares students for active participation in democratic life. Chapter 2 presents the idea of learning talk, highlighting a range of types of learning talk appropriate to English classrooms. It introduces four key dimensions that can shape learning talk in classrooms: contexts and conditions, teacher strategies and practices, types of questions, and student languages. Throughout both chapters, the voices of new English teacher Jackie Loper and her 10th-grade students show what it means to take a dialogic stance in English, in the real world of the classroom. Finally, Part I introduces a metaphor that threads through the book: Teaching is a drafting process that can best be revised and refined through peer collaboration and learning.

# CHAPTER 1

# Why Inspiring Talk Matters

MADISON: I have a question: So why ain't Abigail in jail if she confessed?

TEACHER: That's a great question. So what do we know from watching the end of Act I and Act II?

MICHAELA: Abby acts like she's a victim, and everybody treats her like she is one. Like the afflicted girls are the victims. So, everyone feels sorry for them, and they feel like they have to listen to the afflicted girls because . . .

CAMERON: It seems like Abigail know the answers to everything . . .

TEACHER: Who has given Abigail and the girls the power?

STUDENTS: The people. The whole town.

TEACHER: Which people exactly?

STUDENTS: Parents, ministers.

ANGEL: They supposed to be holy people.

TEACHER: Remember at this time, we're talking about Puritans; we're talking about a theocracy. So who runs Salem?

STUDENTS: The preachers.

MAYA: It's kind of weird that every time the girls react, Abigail be the first one to do somethin'.

This book is about stimulating learning talk about texts in classrooms, the kind of talk Madison, Michaela, Cameron, Angel, and Maya and their 10th-grade English teacher, Jackie Loper, exemplify when they discuss *The Crucible* in the example above. Jackie Loper takes a *dialogic* stance toward her teaching by

- Designing opportunities for students to talk to learn, rather than to display what they have already learned;
- Inviting diverse students to respond to, interact with, and often to disagree with one another, using their own languages;
- Providing space, time, and scaffolding (often in the form of dialogic tools) to help students take responsibility for the direction of classroom talk; and
- Working to learn how students are responding to texts, characters, and ideas so that she can make instructional moves in response to their current thinking.

In classrooms such as Jackie's, where the teacher takes a dialogic stance, students collectively make sense of course content as they contribute meaningfully and substantially to the learning goals at hand.

In culturally and linguistically diverse classrooms, moreover, a dialogic teaching stance frames differences as resources for learning, rather than as problems to overcome. Teachers taking a dialogic stance weave languages—including the African American Language spoken by Angel and Maya—into the life of the classroom. Taking a dialogic stance can thus help to create a more equitable and inclusive classroom learning environment.

Despite its promise for learning, engagement, and educational equity, however, dialogic teaching is not the norm in most schools in the United States. Indeed, going dialogic poses challenges both for the most veteran of teachers and for newcomers to the profession. This book invites teachers both new and veteran to make dialogic teaching part of their ongoing process of learning to teach. It invites teachers to learn with Jackie and many other new teachers, who think carefully about how various teaching practices and dialogic tools can help them engage students' voices and achieve learning goals. It supports teachers in cultivating a flexible pedagogical repertoire, guided by the idea that "what I say responds to what you said."

Before introducing the heart of our argument (in Chapter 2), however, this chapter addresses critical questions you may be asking: Why dialogic teaching now? Aren't schools and classrooms today moving in the opposite direction? We introduce a metaphor for teaching, likening it to an in-process draft fraught with tensions and challenges. Finally, we present the plan for the book.

## WHY DIALOGIC TEACHING NOW?

Dialogic teaching matters for (at least) three key reasons. First, it supports learning. Educational research consistently shows that dialogic teaching supports not only students' literacy learning but also their engagement in that learning. Researchers also show its potential to facilitate greater educational equity in student participation and literacy achievement. Second, dialogic teaching can help teachers navigate the opportunities and challenges of standards such as the Common Core State Standards. Finally, dialogic teaching can play a critical role in advancing the goals of civic engagement and democratic participation.

### Literacy Learning and Engagement

First, let's look at what the research says about the relationship between dialogic teaching and student learning. Research robustly correlates dialogic instructional practices with literacy achievement gains in reading comprehension,

While research is clear on the learning benefits associated with dialogic teaching, certain groups of students are more likely than others to encounter it in school. Some research shows that dialogic teaching occurs less often in urban and rural schools and more often in suburban settings (e.g., Nystrand, 1997). In our work as teacher educators, we often hear teachers worrying that their students cannot handle the responsibility or the cognitive work of such dialogic activities as open-ended dialogue. We especially notice such worries with

- Younger students (e.g., "Maybe upper-level juniors and seniors, but my seventh graders just can't handle it");
- Struggling students (Caughlan & Kelly, 2004); or
- Teachers struggling with classroom management.

Social studies researcher Diana Hess (2009) and literacy researchers Martin Nystrand and colleagues (1997) found that high-tracked and high-socioeconomic status (SES) secondary students were more likely to encounter dialogically organized instruction than low-tracked and low-SES students. Yet students with histories of struggling in school stand to benefit more from discussion-based approaches than do those with higher achievement levels (Kong & Pearson, 2003; Murphy et al., 2009). Dialogic teaching can help to create and sustain more equitable learning environments. Despite these benefits, however, dialogic teaching occurs only rarely in U.S. classrooms (Applebee et al., 2003; Nystrand et al., 1997) and in classrooms around the world (Alexander, 2001).

## Dialogic Teaching and Standardization

In our work as teacher educators, we often hear the question "Who has time for dialogic teaching in an era of high-stakes testing, the Common Core State Standards, and district pacing guides?" Given the research basis outlined above, however, we wonder who doesn't have time for dialogic teaching, given its documented relationship with literacy learning, engagement, and educational equity. Dialogic teaching and standards-based curricula conflict only if teaching to standards means that students do not engage in substantive ways with key disciplinary concepts (e.g., interpretation of literary themes). By *substantive*, we mean that students are talking about curricular content, as opposed to, for example, classroom procedures. Consider your own experience: Do you know anything well that you have not talked about with peers and experts? Mastering a subject matter entails engaging in the disciplinary conversations, talk appropriate and expected in a particular academic discipline or school subject (discussed in more depth in Chapter 2) (Gee, 2008; Langer, 2010; Moje, 2007). These conversations do not take place by listening to the teacher perform them or filling in the blanks on worksheets; students have to engage in learning talk themselves. This argument has long been recognized in England, where high-achieving schools are noted for engaging students in classroom talk and well-sequenced small-group work (Office for Standards in Education, 2011), and where national standards have included attention to formal and informal classroom talk in learning (e.g., Department for Education, 2011).

In the United States, the Common Core State Standards (CCSS) serve as our most recent set of national expectations for learning. The CCSS offer guidelines for speaking and listening skills that we would argue are best developed through dialogic teaching and learning (see text box).

An even greater emphasis of the CCSS—new for some teachers—is teaching students to write arguments that "introduce precise, knowledgeable claim(s), establish the significance of the claim(s), distinguish the claim(s) from alternate or opposing claims, and create an organization that logically sequences claim(s), counterclaims, reasons, and evidence" (CCSS Initiative, 2010, p. 45). Many adults, including those visible in the public sphere, fail to achieve such standards for ar- *argument* gumentation. Yet research suggests that dialogic engagement with the topics of argument can prepare students to write better arguments (Nystrand & Graff, 2001; Reznitskaya, Anderson, & McNurlen, 2001). It follows that teachers should provide classroom practice in argumentative talk with the purpose of helping students to write arguments.

Teaching argument writing is but one example of our broader stance toward standards and specifically the Common Core: Dialogic teaching supports the learning goals laid out in the CCSS. This book further assumes that teachers are "informed professionals" (Luke, Woods, & Weir, 2013) who mobilize the standards as but one resource to support students' learning—alongside their content knowledge, their repertoire of strategies and practices, their knowledge of the students in their classrooms, and their experiences of school and local communities.

---

### What the Common Core State Standards Have to Say About the Range and Content of Student Speaking and Listening

To become college and career ready, students must have ample opportunities to take part in a variety of rich, structured conversations—as part of a whole class, in small groups, and with a partner—built around important content in various domains. They must be able to contribute appropriately to these conversations, to make comparisons and contrasts, and to analyze and synthesize a multitude of ideas in accordance with the standards of evidence appropriate to a particular discipline. Whatever their intended major or profession, high school graduates will depend heavily on their ability to listen attentively to others so that they are able to build on others' meritorious ideas while expressing their own clearly and persuasively. (CCSS Initiative, 2010, p. 48)

## Dialogic Teaching for Democratic Participation

In addition to promoting individual learning, dialogic teaching holds an important place in a functioning democratic society. Learning to dialogue and deliberate with diverse others in school can prepare citizens to capably participate in community and societal dialogues about the pressing issues of our time. Building such capability is an important societal good, especially given how political discourse today is marked by polarized stances, incivility, and impasse on critical issues shaping our future (Moore, 2007; O'Donnell-Allen, 2011).

Debates about issues from healthcare to immigration to climate change reveal how both entrenched inequality and conflicts among different social groups can depress vibrant democratic participation and discourage solutions, often compromises, that advance the common good (Juzwik, Anagnostopoulos, Whyte, Ferkany, & Calabrese-Barton, 2011). When people believe that complex societal problems can best be understood and remedied by experts, who dispense knowledge to dependent citizens, as famously depicted by Freire (1970), they come to feel that they lack control over the problems and questions confronting them. But a consensus is growing that pressing communal and societal issues can best be addressed through open, participatory dialogue and deliberation among diverse constituents (Juzwik et al., 2011). Thus the need for civic—and civil—dialogue in schools has never been more urgent.

Dialogic teaching responds to that need. It thus belongs in a tradition of democratic education dating back to John Dewey (2012). Public school classrooms provide one of the few remaining places in American life where people have sustained opportunities to dialogue about value-laden questions with others who do not share their own ethical frameworks (Hess, 2009; Kunzman, 2006). Dialogic teaching takes advantage of this ideal setting for developing the skills needed for active, civil participation in democratic dialogue and deliberation. Dialogic teaching can especially provide students who identify with groups historically marginalized by unequal civic and political processes with opportunities to express themselves and claim a voice.

Despite the three compelling reasons for dialogic teaching outlined above, dialogue does not happen spontaneously in classrooms, especially given that traditional classroom participation trains students to speak only when they have the right answer. If dialogically organized instruction is not the norm in schools, then teachers and students urgently need to learn, practice, and refine a set of arts and skills for inspiring talk. The following chapters are designed to help you nurture such growth.

## GROWING TOWARD DIALOGIC TEACHING

Taking on dialogic teaching can be a challenging project, even for veteran teachers. The process doesn't immediately result in "the dialogic teacher" and we don't think it should. Perfection isn't the point. New teachers, especially, face numerous challenges as they work to open dialogues in their classrooms. This book illuminates the tensions you may face in your own efforts to harness the power of your students' voices for their literacy learning and development.

## Tensions in Dialogic Teaching

*Taken-for-Granted Terms.* Terms such as discussion and dialogue are familiar and can hold many different meanings. For example, a teacher might use discussion to refer to

- A recitation where he or she does most of the talking,
- A one-on-one conversation with a student, or
- A Socratic seminar where he or she says almost nothing at all.

Because discussion and dialogue are such common terms, we often assume that our middle and high school students know what they mean or that they know how to participate productively in them. In reality, students rarely encounter opportunities to engage in classroom dialogues where *they* are expected to contribute to the language, content, and direction of a lesson. Consequently, open discussions and other dialogic formats rarely just happen on their own. They usually result from careful planning, scaffolding, and facilitation (which involve intense listening). When teachers articulate their terminologies and expectations for themselves and students, when they teach students how to speak to one another, when they deliberately invite student voices into the classroom, students can develop new kinds of learning talk over time.

*Supportive Classroom Environments.* We have already suggested the importance of establishing a supportive classroom environment, but that goal can be confusing. Does being supportive mean that teachers should "accept" all student responses? Does being supportive—combined with the desire to break out of traditional formats of classroom talk—mean that teachers should never evaluate students' responses? What happens when a student gives an inaccurate answer? What happens when a student uses a language form—such as Madison's *ain't*—that can be socially stigmatizing in certain settings? How can you respond when students speak languages unknown to you, such as Navajo, German, or Kiswahili?

Navigating what it means to be supportive is especially tricky when the desire to be supportive starts to feel like "anything goes." On the one hand, being supportive means encouraging students to take risks and to feel safe, to speak up and explore through talk. On the other hand, an anything-goes approach does not usually accomplish the goals of a lesson. How can you be supportive while also correcting inaccuracies? How can you give students the space to explore independently while also teaching them to think critically about unfamiliar ideas?

This book does not advocate an anything-goes approach, but instead helps you assemble a clear understanding of your instructional purpose and goals for student learning talk as you plan lessons.

*Classroom Authority.* The reciprocal aspects of dialogic teaching can present challenges for early career teachers around the issue of authority. For example, some teachers have interpreted the call for reciprocity as a call to take themselves out of discussion, giving up authority in the classroom. When student talk falls flat or when classroom management challenges arise, they question whether dialogic teaching can possibly work for them or for their students. Dialogic teaching does involve students contributing to the direction of classroom talk in a reciprocal relationship with one another and the teacher. It does not, however, mean that teachers should remove themselves from participating in dialogue or exempt themselves from the ultimate responsibility for facilitating dialogue or for effectively managing the classroom. Learning how to assume appropriate authority without taking an authoritarian stance that closes down dialogue is an ongoing challenge for many new teachers who seek to take a dialogic stance as they learn to teach—this book supports you in striking the right balance.

*Unexpected Comments and Questions.* Students respond to lessons and texts in unanticipated ways, and it can be challenging to figure out what to do with such responses in the moment. As a teacher, when should I probe a response further, thus going into depth with an idea? When should I pass over an answer and call on another student, thus eliciting more voices? It can be difficult to know which move to try first. Sometimes it's important to pause and take time to think or observe before responding to an unanticipated answer. The bottom line, however, is that responding to students in the moment does not come with a one-size-fits-all script. Sometimes messy and difficult, such improvisations can also lead to funny, joyful, and memorable interactions. Predicting what might work in different moment-by-moment situations is part of the intellectual inquiry in which teachers can engage across their careers.

This book offers a set of tools for confronting common challenges. Taking a cue from our practices as writing teachers, we also offer a metaphor: Every teaching moment is a *draft* in the composition of your practice (Dawson, 2011). When you think of teaching as drafting work, rather than as performing work, you can transform challenges into opportunities for growth.

## Teaching as a Draft

Following this metaphor, any given lesson is a draft. Viewing lessons as drafts can help you work realistically toward dialogic teaching. Learning to teach involves confronting tensions or dilemmas while "composing a teaching life" (Vinz, 1996) in a real-world classroom where the grittiness of everyday working life can conflict with lofty and academic-sounding ideals like "dialogic teaching." Such process-oriented teaching may seem overly idealistic in a standards-focused landscape where many teachers feel as though they have no room for failure. Yet thinking about teaching as a drafting process allows teachers to embrace both the struggles—the hours of planning, students' unexpected responses in classroom talk, and even teaching missteps—and the gratifying successes as a continuous process of seeing new possibilities, making changes, and learning from initial efforts. On the first page, we introduced you to Jackie and her students, who were puzzling over the characters in *The Crucible*. The transcript was typed by Jackie herself; she videorecorded and transcribed part of her teaching, treating this lesson as a draft in the continued composition of her practice.

Viewing teaching as a draft frames practice not as a final product to be judged but as a work-in-progress to be continually revised and refined. Taking this view of teaching prompts teachers to share works-in-progress with colleagues to solicit feedback and support. Many of our examples will be drawn from new teachers like Jackie—who are working in the context of professional learning communities. In those groups, Jackie and her colleagues share, review, and collaboratively discuss videorecorded clips. In this collaborative video review work, Jackie thinks of each lesson as a first try or a "draft." As she studies videos and transcripts of different drafts from her own and her colleagues' teaching, she imagines other possible moves and responses. She recognizes that her purposes for the lesson do not depend on students' getting the one right answer. What matters more is students' thinking about, working with, and deepening their understanding of how characterization works in the text.

Yet as Jackie makes the shift toward dialogic teaching—a process we will examine further in Chapter 2—she also faces the reality that teaching students to pursue their thinking in an open-ended manner is hard work. Indeed, most students have been drilled across years of schooling to produce the one right answer that the teacher is looking for, a deeply entrenched habit. Because the effort to develop and sustain dialogic teaching is fraught with challenges and tensions, Jackie does not simply try out dialogic practices on her own. Instead, she collaboratively discusses these practices in ways that move her forward as a teacher. Part III of the book will help you engage in such collaborative growth.

## ORGANIZATION OF THE BOOK

We invite you to use the book as a support in going dialogic. You need not read in the order we have organized chapters. You may find it helpful to skip to different sections of the book for different purposes. Throughout the book in every chapter, however, you will encounter classroom examples from new teachers who are going dialogic, in collaboration with their colleagues. Teachers made the transcripts we use from videorecorded lessons they taught during their first year of teaching. To present you with the actual voices of students and teachers, we have chosen not to smooth the transcripts, for example, by removing repetitive words or false starts. Brackets in transcripts show unclear talk, words we added to help the excerpt make sense, or descriptions of nonverbal behaviors. Although the transcripts may not always flow perfectly smoothly, they do authentically show what people said in the classroom. You will also find examples of classroom practice from seasoned veterans, such as Rae Belmont and Lucia Elden, throughout the book. Appendix A categorizes our examples by curricular area and grade level.

Chapter 2 introduces four elements that support taking a dialogic stance to promote learning talk in your classroom: (1) contexts and conditions for dialogic talk across the curriculum, (2) teacher strategies and practices, (3) dialogic questioning processes, and (4) student languages. You will find handouts to use as springboards for talking with students or colleagues about how classroom dialogue is going.

Part II, "Planning for Dialogic Teaching," equips you with some basic planning tools for dialogic teaching across the English language arts curriculum. Chapters focus around different levels of planning in the secondary English language arts curriculum, from daily planning in Chapter 3, to longer-term planning in Chapter 4, to planning in the specific curricular domain of argument writing in Chapter 5.

Part III, "Transforming Practice Through Dialogic Inquiry," introduces classroom discourse analysis (Chapter 6) and video sharing (Chapter 7), two core approaches for learning with others about how to plan for, enact, reflect on, and revise early efforts at dialogic teaching. We hope the final two chapters will offer ideas for continuing growth in formal or informal teacher learning groups, mentoring partnerships, and possibly even give you ideas for a teacher research project or two.

The Coda, "Troubleshooting Common Challenges," addresses issues many encounter in building a repertoire of dialogic practices.

A companion website (vbrr.wiki.educ.msu.edu/) includes book add-ons, reproducibles, questionnaires, sample semester and unit outlines, and other resources that further develop and illustrate ideas in the book. Those interested in the online professional learning communities that inspired this book will find more detailed video and web resources. And those interested in the larger research study grounding the book can find journal articles, conference presentations, and other resources as well (see also Appendix B).

# CHAPTER 2

# Taking a Dialogic Stance to Stimulate Learning Talk

If we want [youth] to talk to learn—as well as learn to talk—
then what they say probably matters more than what
teachers say.

(Robin Alexander, 2008)

## LEARNING ABOUT TALKING TO LEARN

Because students talk to each other before, after, and sometimes during class, and teachers talk all day, it can be easy to forget that *talking to learn*—and specifically how to talk to learn in and about the English language arts—must be *learned*. In schools, teachers teach how to read, write, and use language (e.g., through grammar and vocabulary study). But how well do teachers teach the art of dialoguing with others to advance academic understanding? In some (rare) scenarios, parents and teachers socialize young people into talking to learn in ways that align with dialogic teaching. More typically, however, students have been socialized by years of schooling in which teachers talk and young people listen. Therefore, we consider it a matter of educational equity to plan for and explicitly teach students how to "talk to learn." This chapter introduces four elements that lay a foundation for rich and diverse learning talk: classroom contexts and conditions, repertoires of teaching practices and strategies for talk, the sorts of questions posed to and by students, and students' languages.

Building a dialogic classroom environment from these elements requires taking a dialogic stance. When teachers and students take dialogic stances, as discussed in Chapter 1, they communicate *to each other* sentiments like "I've heard you," "I value what you've said," "I want you to keep talking," and—the sentiment most central to creating and maintaining dialogic environments—"What I say responds to what you've said." In many classrooms, the dialogic stance is partial. For example:

- Students may contribute thoughtfully; however, the "what I say responds to what you've said" stance goes one way, from students to teacher, with no reciprocal move from the teacher in response to students.

13

- A teacher may incorporate students' ideas into her subsequent talk, but the "what I say responds to what you've said" stance rarely circulates among students themselves.

Taking a fully dialogic stance involves learning how to share responsibility with students for how talk unfolds in the classroom.

## WHAT DOES STUDENT
## LEARNING TALK SOUND LIKE?

If you agree on the importance of taking a dialogic stance to stimulate student learning talk, then you might next ask: What might student learning *sound like* in English language arts classrooms? British researcher Robin Alexander (2008) coined the phrase *learning talk* to help answer that question. He also developed a typology of classroom learning talk, which we have adapted in the list below to highlight common types of talk in secondary English. Consider some different kinds of learning talk that you might want to stimulate, depending on your curricular and pedagogical goals.

This list is meant to be generative rather than comprehensive. The important point is that not all learning talk is the same. Learning talk can take a variety of forms that support different instructional goals, from learning new vocabulary words to exploring alternative interpretations of literary characters.

### Speaking Out

*Speculating, imagining, and hypothesizing.* Such talk holds a place of honor in secondary English, where entering imaginatively into literary works is an expected and time-honored disciplinary practice. It can, for example, help students evaluate the choices authors make in crafting a text, specified by the CCSS Reading Standards for Literature, Grades 11–12, nos. 3–5, p. 38 (CCSS Initiative, 2010).

*Narrating.* In this process, students share stories in response to one another or to texts. Often, when teachers or students share stories, that sharing leads to further stories (Juzwik, 2010). Narrating talk can be powerful in literary interpretation or in the process of learning to write narrative.

*Arguing, reasoning, justifying.* Argumentation is an enduring curricular focus in English language arts and other subject areas. Talking to develop and support claims—whether about texts, controversial issues, current events, or other topics—through reasoned argument is a key type of learning talk in English. We'll be exploring arguing talk further in Chapter 5, as we discuss taking a dialogic stance to teaching argument writing.

*Explaining.* Explaining talk may be less frequent in English than in the hard sciences, where much of what students do is explain observed phenomenon. Yet sometimes explaining is called for in English: for example, when students are developing an interpretation or simply clarifying a previous contribution they have made. Explaining talk can sometimes be developed through metaphor or analogy.

*Instructing.* This occurs when students teach one another and sometimes the teacher in their talk. This type of talk can happen during student presentations, where a student has studied something that other students (and even the teacher) have not studied in depth. For example, in preparation for writing a procedural text, students might give a short presentation to peers about how to do something.

*Asking questions.* When students feel comfortable enough to pose questions about course content, that question posing can also offer an excellent indicator of how well students are grasping a concept under study. It can show where they are in the process of learning. This information can, in turn, allow teachers to develop clarifying responses or perhaps even clarifying lessons in response.

*Analyzing and solving problems.* In deliberative talk, for example, when debating the course of action around a controversial policy question, students often need to analyze and generate multiple possible solutions for problems. Group projects and other work in which students have a good deal of autonomy can invite problem-analysis and problem-solving talk.

## It's Your Turn: Dialogic Diagnostic

To begin exploring your own stance toward classroom talk, take the Dialogic Diagnostic (Figure 2.1; also available on the companion website, at vbrr.wiki. educ.msu.edu). You can jot down your answers on a scrap of paper or write in the book. While this multiple choice quiz simplifies the many complicated variables of classroom talk, it also offers an entrée for putting your own beliefs and assumptions about teaching into dialogue with ours. Here are a few questions to discuss with a colleague or two:

- What do I think about the idea of dialogic teaching? Does it go along with or conflict with my goals for student learning in my classroom?
- In what ways do I already take a dialogic stance in my classroom?
- What are some issues related to classroom talk that I'd like to consider further? Are there areas where I know I'd like to work at revising my design for stimulating learning talk?

## Figure 2.1. Dialogic Diagnostic

1.  **When planning, I**

    A.  Always rely on similar patterns of classroom organization no matter the educational goal

    B.  Occasionally mix up the patterns of classroom organization to keep things interesting

    C.  Design diverse tasks and invite specific patterns of classroom organization that align with learning goals

    D.  Always design and use different patterns of classroom organization just to keep things interesting

2.  **I am likely to**

    A.  Change my classroom space around for different learning activities, talk, and purposes once a semester

    B.  Change my classroom space around for different learning activities, talk, and purposes once a month

    C.  Change my classroom space around for different learning activities, talk, and purposes at least once a week

    D.  Find that my room hasn't changed since 1972

3.  **When introducing, transitioning, and concluding lessons, I**

    A.  Always move things along as quickly as possible—there is a lot to cover!

    B.  Provide any need-to-know information before moving on quickly

    C.  Make sure students are oriented to what we are doing/where we are going, while keeping the pace moving to maintain student interest

    D.  Always make sure to give lots of detailed instruction and directions, to the point where I often notice students losing focus

4.  **When I introduce a lesson, I am likely to spend**

    A.  More time on procedures than on ideas

    B.  About as much time on procedures as on ideas

    C.  More time on ideas than on procedures

    D.  No time on ideas or procedures—my students already know the drill

5.  **If a student speaks during a discussion in my class, I am likely to**

    A.  Consider that she has done her work for the day and leave her alone the rest of the class

    B.  Call on her a lot because I know she's prepared

    C.  Nod encouragingly, take occasional notes, and follow up with an invitation to extend and develop her ideas further

    D.  Put a finger to my lips; students don't speak in my class

6. **If I had to put a ratio to the amount students talk in my class versus the amount students write in my class, it would be**

    A.  90% written/10% spoken
    B.  10% written/90% spoken
    C.  50% written/50% spoken
    D.  100% multiple choice quizzes: no speaking or writing

7. **When I picture myself facilitating a discussion, I am likely to be**

    A.  Moving all over the room, gesticulating wildly, getting in students' faces
    B.  At the back of the room, out of the action
    C.  Sitting among students, leaning forward, eyes following the train of conversation, taking occasional notes
    D.  In the teacher's lounge on a coffee break

8. **To teach students how to pose questions, contribute relevant ideas, and listen attentively to others, I**

    A.  Provide a list of desired behaviors at the beginning of the year, then expect them to do what the list says
    B.  Model desired behaviors in my own action, but provide no explicit instruction
    C.  Use a combination of modeling, explicit teaching, and ongoing assessment and feedback to teach desired behaviors
    D.  Don't want students to pose questions, contribute ideas, or listen attentively to their peers; I just want them to listen to me

9. **Through classroom talk, I want students to**

    A.  Show that they can recite the correct answers
    B.  Develop rich and discriminating vocabularies
    C.  Develop a capacity to engage with, and communicate in, different academic registers and genres
    D.  Develop an ability to listen and a will to learn
    E.  B, C, and D above

So how did you do? You probably caught on to the structure of the answer options: A and B are reasonable options in certain situations; C is almost always the most desirable option (except in 9, in which E is the best); and D is largely comic relief (we hope!). What did you learn about yourself and your teaching as a result of doing this diagnostic?

## Taking In

As most know from personal experience, learning talk does not just involve speaking; it also involves listening, considering, and formulating responses to what others say. To learn from others, and to use the ideas of others to advance their own learning, students need to develop skills for weighing what others say.

*Active listening.* In many classrooms, active listening involves making eye contact with the speaker, leaning toward the speaker, nodding in agreement from time to time, and jotting down notes about what is being said. Keep in mind, however, that active listening may take different forms across cultural settings. On the Navajo Nation, for example, adults consider it disrespectful for young people to look them in the eye when they are speaking, so teachers in that setting need to adjust their expectations accordingly.

*Being receptive to multiple alternative viewpoints.* Being receptive to multiple alternative viewpoints is a linchpin of learning from others through dialogue. Close-mindedness to others' viewpoints makes it impossible to learn from them. It may be the case that, for some issues, students are unwilling to countenance alternative viewpoints. If you are teaching a hypothetical unit on argumentation in which students discuss the policy question of marriage rights for same-sex couples, what do you do if one student strongly opposes same-sex marriage for religious reasons? Although the case is complicated, we like Kunzman's (2006) advice: Invite her to articulate her religious ethical framework in response to the questions and issues raised in classroom dialogue, rather than acting as if her religious convictions do not exist.

*Thinking about what is heard and giving others time to think.* It is a truism that in order to learn with, and from, others, students need to mull over and digest what others have to say. To continue with the example of same-sex marriage, this topic may provide an opportunity to work with students on responding to others carefully and deliberately. Sometimes, silence in a discussion can provide that time to think. We sometimes process what we hear in class discussion through note-taking, and students can do the same. In fact, one research study discovered that, during discussions, one quiet student reported that she was making essays in her head (Christoph & Nystrand, 2002)!

Thus far, we have examined what rich student learning talk might sound like. But the more difficult challenge is inspiring such talk in classrooms, day in and day out.

## DRAFTING AND REVISING DISCUSSION: JACKIE'S STORY

To enter into the process of designing and maintaining a classroom environment where rich learning talk is the norm, let's get to know Jackie—whose students were featured at the beginning of Chapter 1—a bit better. While Chapter 1 held up her students' talk as an exemplar of dialogic teaching, this chapter will bring you behind the scenes to show how the level of student learning talk shown in Chapter 1 happened only after months of deliberate effort on Jackie's part.

As a new teacher, Jackie valued discussion, because she saw its potential to help students build meaning and understanding in response to literature. She wanted to use a whole-class discussion to encourage students to analyze characters and to demonstrate various levels of thinking. However, Jackie was discouraged by her first try at whole-class discussion. Students interrupted and talked over one another and a few students dominated the discussion. She found that attempting to get the whole class to interact made classroom management, already a challenge for her, even more difficult than it already was.

Jackie shared a video clip of her teaching with colleagues to help her think about what went wrong in that first discussion. The group noticed that she and her students were having trouble breaking out of a typical pattern of classroom interaction: teacher initiates a question, students respond, then teachers evaluate the response (discussed in the "Types of Teacher Talk in Secondary English" text box on page 22 as recitation). Students tended to raise their hands and wait for her to call on them—as they had learned was appropriate in school. Jackie could see herself slipping into a familiar pattern, doing a lot of summarizing and evaluating but not much taking up or probing students' ideas. Even less was she helping them to take up one another's ideas.

She decided that in her next attempt at discussion, she wanted to support her students in responding to each other's ideas, rather than waiting for their turn, hands up, to respond only to her. She wanted to help them talk to learn.

Following the story of Jackie, a new teacher, illuminates how taking a dialogic stance involves attention to

- Classroom contexts and conditions,
- Strategies and practices for talk,
- Questioning processes, and
- Students' languages.

Tuning in to each of these elements helped Jackie nurture student learning talk.

## CONTEXTS AND CONDITIONS FOR DIALOGIC TEACHING

By the time students reach middle or high school classrooms, many are used to the same patterns of classroom organization no matter the educational goal: Single desks, organized in rows, face frontward, where the teacher presides. The teacher's introductions, transitions, and conclusions in lessons tend to be long and focused on procedures more than on ideas. Students talk very little. Teachers assess them

almost exclusively by what they write versus what they say. And they encounter little to no explicit instruction on, modeling of, or discussion about the communica-
tive norms of the classroom. Some teacher candidates report having played school
using this format from a very young age. According to Alexander (2008), such
patterns have already become entrenched at the elementary level. And they continue into the secondary level. When teachers work to disrupt that status quo in
classrooms, students can get really confused if teachers don't establish, and teach
them how to participate in, a new set of contexts and conditions for talk.

When Jackie looked at contexts and conditions for talk, she realized that she
needed to address some basic problems that were getting in the way. First, the
classroom space—and her own location in that space—needed to be rearranged to
better align with her goal of inviting students' voices to become more prominent.

To prepare for discussion, Jackie and her students arranged the classroom
desks in a circle, where the students could see one another, to align with the goal
of building on each other's ideas. She asked the group to change the hand-rais-
ing norm that they had all learned from many years of schooling. She challenged
them, instead, to listen to one another, to gauge the discussion, and to jump in
when they had something to say. To symbolize her own role in the discussion, she
sat in the circle alongside students. Finally, because whole-group discussion had
presented classroom management challenges in the past, she decided to help students stay focused by assigning their seats.

Jackie realized that she needed to teach her students how to participate, because they had little experience building on one another's ideas in discussions
while at school; rather, they were more familiar with the norm of listening to
teachers and responding when they knew the correct answer. Toward that end,

### Dialogic Tools and the Power of Planning: Insights from Research

Throughout the book, and especially in Part II, we will introduce various
dialogic tools for opening classroom dialogue. In our own research on new
teachers developing dialogic practices, using dialogic tools in planning was
a critical factor for success (Caughlan et al., 2013). While teacher-led tools
were most common, the most powerful tools were student-led tools—where
teachers stepped back and positioned students to interact with content and with
each other, thus sharing responsibility for the direction of classroom interaction.
Some examples of student-led dialogic tools are debate, fishbowl, gallery walk,
literature circles, Socratic seminar, unscripted drama activities, role-playing
games, some forms of small-group work, and think-pair-share, all discussed
further in Chapter 3.

she needed to furnish her students with some *tools* for participating in classroom dialogue. This book will introduce various *dialogic tools*: practical tools mobilized in planning and practice, with potential to generate rich learning talk.

One such tool Jackie used was an envisionment builder discussion sheet with questions, including those listed below, to guide students through an increasingly more complex interpretation of Act II of Arthur Miller's *The Crucible* (Langer, 1995):

- *Initial Thoughts:* What questions came to mind?
- *Developing Ideas:* How did your understanding of Mary Warren change throughout Act II? What do you think she will do in Act III: tell the truth or continue to lie?
- *Learning from the Text:* What social issues does *The Crucible* make you think about today?
- *Taking a Critical Stance:* Do you think the movie or the play paint a more accurate portrait of Puritan lifestyle in the 1690s?

The envisionment builder, gleaned from studying Adler and Rougle (2005), encouraged students to note thoughts and experiences while reading. As she planned the lesson, Jackie reasoned that first jotting down their thoughts on the play might provide them with material to contribute to the discussion. The full version of Jackie's envisionment builder discussion sheet can be found on the companion website (vbrr.wiki.educ.msu.edu).

The discussion sheet invited exploratory writing intended to help students think, talk, and learn about *The Crucible*. The sheet did not assess what they already knew or ask them for the teacher's interpretation of the play. Jackie introduced this writing as preparation for discussion, rather than introducing discussion as preparation for writing. In this way, she changed the relationship between writing and talking so common in secondary English classrooms.

## BEYOND RECITATION:
## STRATEGIES AND PRACTICES FOR CULTIVATING DIALOGIC TALK

Many teachers like Jackie struggle to figure out the teacherly moves that will help them move beyond entrenched ways of doing secondary English, including typical kinds of teacher talk dominating most classrooms (see text box).

What strategies empower teachers to move beyond default practices like procedures and directions, read-aloud, lecture, and recitation? What strategies create richer possibilities for student learning talk? Jackie employed 10 key strategies and practices in her second attempt at discussion. You can find a full transcript of Jackie's classroom interaction and other resources on our website (vbrr. wiki.educ.msu.edu).

## A Closer Look: Types of Teacher Talk in Secondary English

Among the types of teacher talk that occur in secondary English classrooms in the United States are the following:

- Procedures and Directions: Teacher tells students what to do or explains how to do it
- Read-Aloud: Teacher reads a text aloud to students
- Lecture: Teacher explains or models a concept or process, presents information, and so on
- Recitation: Teacher poses or initiates questions, students respond to questions, and teachers evaluate student answers (initiate, respond, evaluate, or the IRE sequence) (e.g., Mehan, 1979)
- Deliberation: Students and teacher exchange ideas to collaboratively address/solve problems or achieve goals
- Dialogue: Students and teacher attempt to achieve common understanding "through structured and cumulative questioning and discussion" (Alexander, 2008, p. 38)

While the first four types of talk are most pervasive in U.S. classrooms, the second two are less widely used. Yet scholars document that the latter two are especially powerful tools for student learning (e.g., Alexander, 2008; Nystrand, 1997). Both deliberation and dialogue can involve open discussion, where three or more students and teacher talk together for 30 seconds or more (Nystrand, 1997, p. 36).

*Design questions to provoke thoughtful responses.* As she developed the discussion sheet, Jackie posed questions to provoke thoughtful responses (see above), rather than testing for one right answer. She then mobilized those questions to open the discussion. For example, her first entry into the conversation reminded students of a question she had scripted on the discussion sheet:

> So, look at your answers for developing ideas number 1. So read that, and then let's talk about Mary Warren for a little bit.

Jackie's reference back to the question ("How did your understanding of Mary Warren change throughout Act II? What do you think she will do in Act III: tell the truth or continue to lie?") and to students' earlier thinking about that question opened up an animated and thoughtful conversation.

*Treat students' responses to questions as conversational building blocks.*
Throughout the discussion, Jackie built on students' thoughts and responses to
collaboratively move the discussion forward.

> MICHAELA: I think that she may tell the truth. I think at first maybe she
> might like think about it—like should I tell the truth, should I not? But
> I think she will tell the truth. If she doesn't, she's a poor [inaudible] . . .
> Um, I think she might.
> TEACHER: So, you have faith in Mary Warren to tell the truth.
> JAMIE: I don't think so. I think Abby . . . If he [Proctor] got all up in my
> face like that I'd be like, "All right then, sir, I'll tell the truth . . ." [other
> inaudible responses].
> MAYA: I think Abigail's gonna tell the truth.
> TEACHER: Do you think Abigail's going to tell the truth, Maya?
> MAYA: Yeah.

By contrast, a more typical, unconnected question-and-answer session would feature a teacher asking a prescripted question; students answering it; and the teacher
moving on to the next question on her list, regardless of how the students an-
swered the first question.

*Collaborate with students to connect exchanges into coherent curricular
conversations.* This one discussion was thematically connected to a unit-long exploration of the big ideas of "intolerance, hysteria, and the power of the individual" in the context of *The Crucible* and related texts.

*Encourage students to ask questions and provide explanations.* Sometimes
Jackie simply revoiced or articulated the implication of what someone else had
previously said, for example:

> CAMERON: I think she's probably going to change her mind at the last
> minute and then that's when it's like they don't know what to believe.
> TEACHER: Okay, so maybe she's going to change her story so much that no
> one knows what to believe.

At other times, she explicitly cued explanations and questions, as in "What do you
guys think?"

*Speak in a clear and animated voice.* Students could hear Jackie clearly
throughout the discussion. Because she sat in the circle with them, they could also
see her and her gestures clearly without having to peer over other students' heads.

*Practice disciplinary talk in English.* A key goal for the lesson was to "analyze the characters in Act II," an enduring curricular goal in English language arts and one that shows up in the CCSS: "Analyze how complex characters (e.g., those with multiple or conflicting motivations) develop over the course of a text, interact with other characters, and advance the plot or develop the theme" (CCSS Initiative, 2010, p. 36). Jackie kept her pedagogical goals in focus by using tools that allowed her to share responsibility with students for probing characters' actions, motivations, and development in Act II of *The Crucible*.

*Work to balance broad participation with in-depth exploration of ideas.* While the participation wasn't as broad as Jackie would have liked (as we will see below), Jackie and her students did go in depth with ideas about various characters and their interactions with one another. More generally, the balance between the depth of ideas explored and the breadth of participation can be tricky. While some teachers make it their goal for every student to participate in discussions, it is also important that curricular content be explored in depth. Sacrificing depth of ideas for breadth of participation can pose problems in terms of staying focused on learning goals. Some teachers use the strategy of first inviting a wide range of responses to students' "initial understandings," a term Jackie learned from Adler and Rougle's (2005) textbook on dialogic instruction (derived from Langer, 1995). They then build on responses from students raising ideas or issues that warrant—in the teacher's judgment, and this *is* a judgment call—further exploration or elaboration.

*Help students see errors as opportunities to learn.* Jackie led her students to collaboratively think out loud, to talk in an exploratory way, rather than only to display that they had the "right answer." In order to engage in such talk, students needed to feel comfortable that the teacher wouldn't "mark them down" for getting a wrong answer. In fact, the incessant focus on getting the right answer can deprive students of an opportunity to engage with a key aspect of disciplinary talk in English: generating, developing, comparing, and critiquing multiple textual interpretations. Sometimes students build those interpretations in response to texts the class has read, and other times with reference to other students' or their own writing.

Several reproducibles on the website (vbrr.wiki.educ.msu.edu/) offer tools for talking about and reflecting with colleagues and students about these strategies and practices.

Jackie herself reflected on how her second try at discussion went, after viewing a video clip:

> While I sat in the circle, I jotted down notes of which students were talking and the gist of what they said. I also structured this discussion differently than the last in that I told the students that they didn't need to raise their

## Disciplinary Talk in English: How Does Talk in English Compare to Talk in Other Secondary Subject Areas?

Talk in English differs from that in disciplines like mathematics, which are characterized by consensus about various principles. Consider, for example, the difference between the historically agreed upon rules for working with negative numbers in mathematics and the open-ended analysis of characters in a literary work such as *The Crucible* in English (but keep in mind that literary studies is but one subdiscipline within the broader discipline of English). In mathematics, students work to understand and apply fundamental principles, for example: negative number times negative number equals positive number. In literary studies, on the other hand, classroom talk and the reasoning processes underlying it tend to emphasize

- Establishing what happened to characters or what characters do or have done (comprehending the plot line);
- Generating multiple perspectives on and interpretations of what happened;
- Imaginatively empathizing with and critically examining characters' motivations and actions;
- Studying how authors use linguistic, stylistic, generic, and other conventions to animate different characters across the work(s); and
- Comparing the nature of problematic situations that characters find themselves in and how they act in those situations.

Rich literary works, such as *The Crucible*, tend to be interpretively ambiguous. Most literary scholars today would agree that no historically agreed upon "right answer" or principle for students to learn and apply in studying *The Crucible* has already been settled, as might be the case in mathematics talk.

While some might choose to take a more closed stance toward literary studies, treating the discipline as an established set of principles or information for students to master (e.g., symbolism, plot, and so on), that stance does not align with the disciplinary practices in the academic discipline of literary studies. When teachers do take the more open stance toward disciplinary talk in English, it tends to have quite a lot in common with talk in social studies, especially history, civics, geography, and anthropology. As a result, learning from colleagues and research in social studies education can help English teachers refine skills and get new ideas for leading classroom talk, for example, about controversial issues (Hess, 2009) or historical events (Juzwik, 2013).

hands, and I encouraged the discussion phrases on the board [note: The discussion phrase tool is discussed in Chapter 3]. I really tried to stay out of the conversation a bit more than last time because I realized that I . . . needed to allow them to talk to each other more.

Upon reviewing my notes and watching this clip, I can definitely see that there are some students dominating this discussion. I have a few ideas of how to encourage more participation. . . . Also, only some students followed the discussion phrases so how can I encourage them to begin with these without interrupting them/stifling their contributions?

Jackie comments that her primary role during the discussion involved jotting down notes about who was talking and what was being said. This recording work kept her busy enough to "stay out of the conversation a bit more," although she did not remove herself altogether—and given her instructional goal of working on character analysis and interpretation, that choice made sense. Her role implies that she is embracing a fuller dialogic stance.

Jackie's reflection indicates that she sees her lesson as a draft. In future drafts, Jackie builds on her past experiences to make revisions that further fine-tune her dialogic strategies and practices. She focuses on a problem area she sees (and a classic problem for many teachers who use discussion-based teaching strategies): vocal participation by a limited number of students. Upon reflection, she wonders how to invite broader participation without sacrificing the depth of ideas shown in the discussion—a balance that can be difficult for even the most experienced teachers to strike. Another strategy for broadening participation is inviting students to help manage turn taking, for example, through shared routines like using a pass toy to designate speakers or calling on the next speaker after making their contribution.

Many teachers identify dialogic teaching with the practice of having whole-class discussions, like Jackie (herself influenced by the mentor text by Adler and Rougle, 2005). As we point out above, however, different learning goals require different types of interactions, including

- Teacher-student group interactions (e.g., teacher-led discussion);
- Student-to-student interactions (e.g., small-group work); and
- teacher-to-student one-on-one monitoring (e.g., writing conferences).

No instructional format or dialogic tool—even if that format is open discussion—is universally or inherently a "best practice" or even a good practice. The benefit of any practice or tool should rather be determined in light of the goals for a given lesson and the skills, interests, and dynamics of students in a given classroom setting.

For Jackie's goal of helping her students study characterization, the open discussion format made sense. Chapter 3 introduces a set of dialogic tools for different ways of structuring classroom talk. Across these instructional formats, the set of teaching strategies and practices introduced above, especially when used in combination, can invite students' voices into the classroom in powerful ways that promote learning across the curriculum of English language arts.

## QUESTIONING PROCESSES FOR TALKING TO LEARN

How teachers structure questions, whether in writing or in the flow of classroom talk itself, can be crucial to whether or not dialogic talk flourishes. We can think about the process in terms of posing questions, responding to questions, and responding to responses. While teacher questions matter, student questions are one of the most important resources for inspiring talk.

### Posing Questions

The text box below shows four different types of questions that can occur in classrooms. When teachers and students take up a previous comment in posing a new question or making a new comment, they encourage cumulative talk. Authentic questions can give students opportunities to reciprocally and collaboratively explore ideas "out loud." When teachers create conditions for student questions to flourish and shape the direction of subsequent talk, they build a classroom climate of *collaboration* and *support*.

Taking a dialogic stance in the questions teachers pose to students can involve:

- Giving students time to think (wait time) when they pose questions;
- Combining routine and probing questions; and
- Balancing invitations for known-answer and authentic questions.

If you work with the transcript from Jackie's discussion (available at vbrr.wiki. educ.msu.edu), you will find that most of Jackie's questions are authentic. In one exchange with Maya, her question simply revoices Maya's contribution:

MAYA: I think Abigail's gonna tell the truth.
TEACHER: Do you think Abigail's going to tell the truth, Maya?

In the flow of this conversation, such repetition serves as uptake that follows student ideas to keep the conversation moving. In the discussion sheet on the website, you will find that some of the questions are "routine"—meaning they could be asked about any work. For example, "What questions come to your mind?" (Question 3). But *none* is a known-answer question; all are authentic. They work as heuristics to elicit students' ideas and spur thinking. Because of the focus on prompting student thinking, dialogic questioning requires giving students time to think after questions are posed, even if silence may initially feel uncomfortable.

## A Closer Look: A Taxonomy of Classroom Question Types

- *Known–Answer/Test Question:* Questions for which the asker knows the answer, but is testing to see if the person answering knows the "right" answer. Also called test questions, as they replicate in talk the sort of questions that might appear on a test or quiz.

     TEACHER: Who has given Abigail and the girls the power?

- *Authentic Question:* Questions for which the asker does not know the answer but is curious to know what or how the person answering thinks about it. Whether or not a question is authentic often depends on the background knowledge of those expected to answer it.

     TEACHER: What do you guys think?

- *Uptake Question:* Questions resulting when the question-asker takes up a previous contribution (often an answer to an earlier question) in order to formulate a new question. Uptake is usually indicated by a pronoun (that), by word repetition (question), or by a transition word (so)—in the case below, all three. Many teachers find uptake a powerful tool for building cumulative learning talk in classrooms.

     MADISON: I have a question: So why ain't Abigail in jail if she confessed?
     TEACHER: That's a great question. So what do we know from watching the end of Act I and Act II?

- *Student Question:* Questions resulting when a student, rather than the teacher, poses a question. When they occur, student questions are almost always authentic. Student questions can be especially powerful tools for sparking dialogues (Nystrand et al., 2003).

     TAHARA: If everybody turns on her then, what will Betty do? Will she stay? She was the one that started it so . . . what is she gonna do?

Known-answer—or test—questions dominate U.S. secondary English classrooms, not to mention classrooms of all subjects and ages the world over (Alexander, 2008; Nystrand, 1997). Many educational researchers over the years have lamented the prominence of known-answer questions (e.g., Mehan, 1979; Nystrand, 1997). Others, however, argue—we think persuasively—that taking a dialogic stance depends less on a question being authentic and more on whether a question (1) responds to previous talk and (2) stimulates cumulative talk and reasoning (Alexander, 2008; Boyd & Markarian, 2011). Nonetheless, authentic questions can indicate a dialogically oriented environment in secondary English classrooms.

## Responding to Questioning

In the typical recitation format, teachers look for brief "right" answers, so that they can move on to their next question or point without pausing. Taking a dialogic stance, however, invites us to consider other goals for questioning:

> Goal 1: In-depth response
> Goal 2: Extended student talk
> Goal 3: Wide participation (as many students speaking
>         as possible)

In-depth responses to questions generate further commentary and exploration. Sometimes, those responses pose further problems or additional questions. Consider, for example, this exchange:

> TEACHER: So, look at your answers for developing idea number 1. So read that, and then let's talk about Mary Warren for a little bit. In Act II we saw how Mary Warren was reacting to all of this.
>
> CAMERON: Um, I think she will continue to lie because of the fact that she is so afraid that Abigail will turn against her and call her a witch and then she don't wanna be hanged or either go to jail and then like I just think what she's doing is a big mistake because it's like even still she is taking someone else's life because she's grown—the lady's grown—so she might be hanged for that. So, it's like—she not even thinking, really—like she's more afraid so she's not gonna do the right thing. But, I think she's probably going to change her mind at the last minute and then that's when it's like they don't know what to believe.

It may seem that Jackie isn't exactly posing a question here; however, she is inviting students to collaboratively think "in depth." Because of its function as an invitation to talk about a specific topic, and because of its invocation of a question they'd already considered, we would classify the teacher utterance as a question. That question invites in-depth response and exploration—talking to learn. The long student turn elicited by that invitation (123 words) is noteworthy, because "extended talk" by students in classrooms is rare, even though such talk can transform knowledge and understanding (Thompson, 2008).

Let's consider a final issue about responding to questioning: How do you respond to student questions, when they do occur? The answer depends on the goal of the lesson, of course, but we generally counsel teachers (ourselves included) to resist the temptation to quickly jump in and answer the question. For example, consider Jackie's response to Tahara's question:

> TAHARA: If everybody turns on her then, what will Betty do? Will she stay? She was the one that started it so . . . what is she gonna do?
> JACKIE: What do you guys think?

Jackie supports the question by turning it back to the class. In addition to valuing student inquiry and curiosity, teacher silence in this context can create space for students to think more deeply together.

## Responding to Responses

In the typical recitation framework, teachers pose known-answer questions, students answer, and teachers then give them feedback about whether they are right or wrong. Taking a dialogic perspective complicates the teacher's work of responding to student responses, because the goal is less to evaluate or provide feedback on the student's answer and more to "sustain lines of inquiry" (Alexander, 2008). Here are a few rules of thumb for responding to student responses:

*Avoid habitual praise and use recognition strategically.* Habitual praise means saying something complimentary, like "very good," every time someone responds to a question you pose. Such praise quickly becomes meaningless. If you find it difficult to break the habit, try using the more neutral "okay" to acknowledge when students make contributions, with the goal of eventually eliminating such verbal tics that get repeated every time students respond to questions. Verbal recognition can be very powerful, however, when used strategically to describe back to students the dialogic moves (and other successful behaviors) you see them accomplishing. For more ideas about praise talk and the power of recognizing successful student behaviors, see Glasser and Easley (2008) and Johnston (2012, especially Chapter 4).

*Avoid simple judgment and routine revoicing.* Avoiding judgment and routine revoicing can shift the teacher role from *evaluator* of student thinking to *sustainer* of student thinking. Keep in mind, however, that sometimes revoicing or paraphrasing a previous student comment can sustain dialogue, for example:

> MICHAELA: I kinda disagree with that; I think that she may tell the truth. I think at first maybe she might like think about it—like should I tell the truth, should I not? But I think she will tell the truth. If she doesn't, she's a poor [inaudible] . . . Um, I think she might.
> TEACHER: So, you have faith in Mary Warren to tell the truth.
> VARIOUS STUDENTS: I don't think so. I think Abby . . . If he [Proctor] got all up in my face like that I'd be like, "All right then, sir, I'll tell the truth . . ." [other inaudible responses].

When Jackie paraphrases Michaela's contribution, it leads to further development of student ideas. She used revoicing strategically, to probe an issue that seemed debatable and therefore likely to generate deeper thinking about the character.

*Offer informative or generative feedback on which students can build.* Sometimes feedback may simply state a point of information from a text under study or elsewhere. Sometimes it may offer a more in-depth analysis of a problem or implication raised by the comment, as in "Does what you are suggesting imply . . . ?"

## TAKING A DIALOGIC STANCE TOWARD STUDENTS' LANGUAGES

Taking a dialogic teaching stance means not only respecting and responding to what students say (the content of their talk), but also valuing *how* they speak. Students' own languages (Conference on College Composition and Communication, 1974), including those spoken, written, performed, or otherwise communicated in and out of classrooms, can be a critically important component of classroom learning talk. Students' own languages might be indigenous languages such as Cherokee or Navajo (e.g., Cushman, 2012); immigrant and refugee languages such as Spanish and Hmong (e.g., Duffy, 2011); second languages such as Mandarin Chinese or Dominant American English (DAE); heritage languages such as Arabic (Sarroub, 2005); historically hybridized languages such as African American Language (e.g., Smitherman, 1977); or dialects such as Appalachian English (e.g., Purcell-Gates, 1997). Students' languages have received heightened political and educational attention in recent years as some states have outlawed them in classrooms by mandating that only DAE be allowed. These developments work against the logic of the dialogic stance we are promoting, because they assert that ways of speaking that diverge from DAE are without value—an assumption that, in turn, devalues student identities and ideas. If the only acceptable language in a classroom is DAE, then it limits who can participate. Insisting on DAE also limits students' participation, because talking to learn becomes impossible when attempting to revise one's oral language at the same time. By contrast, taking a dialogic stance involves valuing and supporting students' languages, even while expanding their repertoires of discourse into new directions.

Taking a dialogic stance further entails designing classroom environments where linguistic norms and practices are shaped by the language practices of the students, not just those of the teacher.

Jackie's linguistically diverse classroom provides an opportunity to think more deeply about students' languages, although it does not include examples of student languages unfamiliar to the teacher. As the discussion we've already studied continued to unfold, student languages became resources for deepening understanding and moving the conversation forward. Three examples from the Chapter 1 transcript may raise concern for those who insist that only DAE should be spoken by students in classrooms.

First comes Madison's question: "I have a question: So why ain't Abigail in jail if she confessed?" The usage in question is the word *ain't*, a word often viewed pejoratively by DAE speakers but often used in the African American Language

(AAL) and rural dialects spoken by families in the community where Jackie's classroom was located. Several aspects of the interaction surrounding that contribution relate to taking a dialogic stance. First, Jackie validates the contribution through her response, "That's a great question." She next builds on it in formulating a question of her own: "So what do we know [about that] from watching the end of Act I and Act II?" She thus provides a scaffold or encouragement for other students to engage the question. She certainly does not correct the informal, some would say "incorrect" or "low-status" usage, because that would have (1) demeaned the value of the students' contribution and (2) derailed the opportunity for substantive discussion about characterization that was opened by a great question about the text.

Two further examples involve AAL. For example, a few turns later, Jackie asks, "Who has given Abigail and the girls the power?" and "Which people exactly?" One response is the perceptive remark, "They supposed to be holy people." The construction "they supposed" is a typical feature of AAL (what linguists call the *zero copula*), where the speaker chooses to eliminate a *to be* verb. Jackie builds on the student's contribution when she articulated the theocracy idea. Maya also deploys the "habitual be" feature of AAL: "Every time the girls react, *Abigail be* the first one to do something." She chooses to use an invariant *be* (rather than the less precise DAE *is*) to mark habitual actions in the present tense. Her comment spurs further interpretation by another student. In both cases, students collaboratively learn through speaking in their own languages—and we think this freedom should be extended to other languages, including those unfamiliar to the teacher. Encouraging multilingual learning talk can prepare students not only to make their voices heard, but also to productively listen to those who speak other languages in a linguistically pluralistic world. To further deepen students' speaking and listening capacities, consider discussing the opportunities and challenges such talk presents. Students may have an opportunity to gain familiarity with a new language or to process a difficult new idea in a shared language with a partner who also speaks that language. Multilingual learning talk may also push students and teacher alike to confront certain challenges, such as translation. The meta-lessons discussed in Chapters 3 and 4 can be a great tool for deepening students' language awareness in classroom talk.

The bottom line: To make talking to learn a top priority in English classrooms, it only makes sense to encourage students to participate and contribute just as they are, not as idealized students reciting what they already know or what the teacher wants to hear, in DAE. In many cases, students can learn much more through participation in heritage languages than they would through participation in DAE. Indeed, facilitating public school classroom and school environments of openness to students' languages and hybridizations may help play a small part in facilitating higher-quality civil discourse across diverse cultural and linguistic groups in our society.

# PART II

# Planning for
# Dialogic Teaching

As you learned in Part I, research and scholarship offer many compelling reasons to engage students in dialogic learning talk: It supports literacy achievement gains, equitable educational outcomes, and students' capacities for democratic participation. However, dialogic practices remain rare in classrooms today. Experienced and new teachers alike face steep challenges when they aspire to go against the grain of historically dominant classroom practices—such as lecture and recitation. Many encountered such teaching practices as students. Many did well in school and thus feel comfortable with the status quo. However, teacher-dominated forms of classroom talk are not sufficient to engage students in the types of discussion and complex thinking needed for argument writing and the reading of more complex texts demanded by 21st-century literacies and standards, including the Common Core.

Just knowing about the importance of dialogic teaching and talking to learn doesn't magically make it happen. Planning is essential. Our research with new teachers found that using dialogic tools in planning was closely associated with higher student participation. Purposeful planning for engagement in talking to learn disrupted the status quo classroom discourse practices of both students and teachers.

This section provides you with tools for achieving the types of teacher moves and learning talk described in Chapter 2. Chapter 3 offers a set of dialogic tools for English teaching and shows how they can be combined and sequenced within daily lessons. Chapter 4 provides a template for planning for ever-more-dialogic instruction over the course of a semester or year, in the process showing how such planning can align with curricular standards. Chapter 5 illustrates how to align classroom talk and writing assignments to support students' argument writing. Contrasting two different frameworks for approaching argument, we show how taking a dialogic stance involves fundamentally rethinking argument writing assignments and instruction from a dialogic perspective—an approach we call conversational entry.

# CHAPTER 3

# Planning Day by Day:
# Dialogic Tools for Inspiring Talk

Have you ever set out to fix an incredible meal? You go online, you find a recipe, you invite the guests, you buy all the ingredients, you don your apron, you find your favorite cooking music, and you read the first recipe instruction: "Zest your lemons and combine with 3 tablespoons of lemon juice." And then you realize you don't have a zester or a juicer.

Overlooking the tools required to produce our desired outcome can be disastrous in both the kitchen and the classroom. Planning carefully in order to make sure you have the appropriate tools handy, on the other hand, can help you accomplish your teaching and learning goals. As with recipes, the simple verbs used in directions can mask the tools and complex steps necessary to accomplish a task. *To zest* requires a *zester*. And often *to discuss* requires more than the students' mouths and ability to form words—it requires attention to sequence and detail and the appropriate tools to enact your plans. In this chapter, we describe how planning—while being mindful of the tools you'll need to meet your goals—can make or break your dialogic dinner party.

## WHAT IS A DIALOGIC TOOL?

A dialogic tool is an activity, heuristic, assemblage, guide, or other mechanism a teacher uses in planning and practice that helps scaffold students into talking to learn. Those tools range from arranging desks in a circle, to a Socratic seminar, to an online discussion board prompt.

### Tools Support Talking to Learn

Using dialogic tools designed to elicit student voices can significantly increase student participation and can reshape the ways teachers conduct a class (Caughlan et al., 2013). In our research on new teachers going dialogic, we found that teachers who called upon dialogic tools in planning were more likely than those who didn't to inspire learning talk in their classrooms. Two specific dialogic teacher moves correlated with dialogic tool use—uptake and authentic questions. Uptake, and

*Student ideas shape learning*

cumulative talk more generally, are key indicators of classrooms where student ideas shape learning (Boyd & Galda, 2011), as established in Chapter 2. Teachers using dialogic tools were also more likely to pose authentic questions (for which the teacher does not have a "right answer" in mind) to students, another indicator of dialogically oriented learning environments discussed in Chapter 2.

## The Toolbox

Table 3.1 and Table 3.2 illustrate dialogic tools that teachers we've worked with have used in planning. The list is not comprehensive. Rather, the table offers a collection of tools that you can use to promote talking to learn in your classroom. We encourage you to add tools from your own experience that can be used dialogically.

We've categorized the tools in a couple of different ways. First, we've broken them down according to who leads them and when they might be used:

*Who:* Is the tool teacher led or student led? and
*When:* Is the tool used to . . .
- Prepare students for talking to learn;
- Practice talking to learn; or
- Reflect on an experience of talking to learn?

## TOOLS AND THEIR FUNCTIONS

### Teacher-Led Tools

While it is true that one of the ultimate goals of dialogic instruction is to help students participate independently in more student-led and student-centered talk, it is also true that achieving high-quality student-led talk results from deliberate and scaffolded instruction over time. As students learn to take more and more responsibility for classroom talk, you play an important role in generating, facilitating, and participating in that talk. Teacher-led tools can be powerful for

- Making your role explicit;
- Supporting you in breaking out of the typical recitation pattern; and
- Planning thoughtfully for student talk.

Teacher-led tools are tools you, the teacher, create or adapt that allow you to maintain primary responsibility for directing the flow of classroom dialogue. That dialogue may occur verbally, for example, in an open discussion, or through written text, such as in journal prompts. Other examples of teacher-led tools include comprehension games, Four Corners, or authentic questions that you have scripted in advance.

*p 38*

# Table 3.1. Teacher-Led Tools

Teachers develop or adapt, then implement and maintain responsibility for direction of classroom talk.

| Tool Name and Description | When to Use |
|---|---|
| *Student Writing That Prepares for Talk* | |
| ANTICIPATION GUIDE<br><br>A set of statements or questions about which students will likely have strong feelings and about which students can reasonably disagree. You provide students with a short worksheet or questionnaire to fill out in preparation for discussion. Because the statements or questions "anticipate" major themes of a text or unit, you can use anticipation guides as a pre-reading activity to pique interest, to activate prior knowledge, or to scaffold critical thinking. | Prepare |
| COMPOSING PROMPT<br><br>An opportunity for students to write (either individually or collaboratively) in response to a question, idea, statement or quote. For example, students can draft an answer to an interpretive question or they can do personal journal writing. Not all composing prompts are dialogic tools, but can be when used to give students time to develop individual thinking to prepare for small-group or large-group talk. | Prepare |
| *Teacher Writing That Prepares for Talk* | |
| TEACHER-SCRIPTED QUESTIONS<br><br>Questions teachers prepare in advance of a lesson. Teacher-scripted questions generally target ideas and objectives teachers want to address in recitation or discussion. A dialogic tool when used to create opportunities for student learning talk. | Prepare |
| RUBRIC<br><br>A set of outlined expectations regarding type, quantity, or quality of participation. A teacher-led tool when you compose and distribute it. | Prepare, Practice, Reflect |
| WORKSHEET<br><br>A hard copy of questions or activities. A dialogic tool when it promotes independent or small-group thinking and talk about a concept, or when it includes authentic or uptake questions. | Prepare, Practice, Reflect |

*(continued)*

Table 3.1. *(continued)*

*for middle*
*school's going to*
*b4 going have*
*corners, pair decide*
*them up + by discussing 1st*

| Tools to Promote Talk-in-Interaction | |
|---|---|
| FOUR CORNERS<br><br>Teacher reads a set of controversial statements or open-ended questions. Students decide whether they strongly agree, somewhat agree, somewhat disagree, or strongly disagree with each statement. Students physically move to the corner of the classroom representing one of the four positions. You can facilitate a large-group discussion by asking students from each corner to dialogue about their stances and interpretations. | Practice |
| TAKE A STAND<br><br>A controversial topic is presented along with varying stances on the topic. Much like "Four Corners," this activity invites students to agree or disagree on an issue or topic. You can ask students to spatially represent their "stand" by moving to different sides of the room. | Practice |
| SHARING READING STRATEGIES<br><br>Making reading social and public through explicit sharing of strategies and background knowledge in a group setting. This practice helps struggling readers see how it's done and helps everyone stay motivated. | Prepare, Reflect |
| TEACHER TOKENS<br><br>Small objects used by the teacher to randomly select the next speaker, such as slips of paper in a jar. You can use tokens to make sure students distribute turns at talk. | Practice |
| *Writing in Response* | |
| REFLECTION/SELF-ASSESSMENT<br><br>Students assess or reflect on their own or others' dialogic participation. Students can gain awareness of what they have learned about content and about the process of talking to learn, and you can gain a vantage point on students' learning processes. | Reflect |

*You can find examples of the tools throughout the book and on our companion website (vbrr.wiki.educ.msu.edu.)

# Table 3.2. Student-Led Tools

Teachers step back and position students to interact with content and with each other, thus sharing responsibility for direction of classroom interaction.

| Tool and Description | When to Use |
|---|---|
| *Tools to Organize Interaction* | |
| DEBATE<br><br>An activity structured to put students on opposite sides of a controversial issue or question. Debates vary widely in style, but most are formal and highly structured to offer students on each side equal opportunities for stating or countering arguments. | Prepare, Practice |
| FISHBOWL<br><br>A small portion of the class discusses in a circle at the center, while the rest of the group listens to that discussion from a larger circle around the outside. You can use the center discussion to model high-quality discussion, to share small-group collaboration with the larger group, or to encourage listeners in the outer circle to reflect on the activity in the center. | Practice, Reflect |
| GALLERY WALK<br><br>Quotes, artifacts, questions, or examples of work are posted around the room. Students stroll around to browse them. You can have students stop by artifacts that are particularly interesting to them and articulate (through writing or talking) the meaning or interest behind it. | Practice |
| LITERATURE CIRCLE<br><br>A small collaborative group of students who read a text and meet together to conduct their own discussion and analysis of it. Literature circle protocols can be highly structured or relatively open. You or students can select the texts. | Practice |
| SOCRATIC SEMINAR<br><br>A large-group, student-led discussion around a text. You establish the rules and expectations in advance, and students come prepared with questions and ideas to share. Many teachers try to minimize their participation. | Prepare, Practice |

*(continued)*

Table 3.2. *(continued)*

| | |
|---|---|
| PAIR SHARE<br><br>A discussion between two students. In pairs, students briefly share ideas about a text, question, or lesson. This exercise invites students to collaboratively "think out loud" during a lesson. You can follow up by inviting pairs to share with the larger group. | Prepare, Practice |
| SMALL-GROUP WORK<br><br>Collaboration among three or more students. Depending on your purpose and on student experience, you can design group-work along a continuum of more-structured to less-structured (to support growing student autonomy). Structures for small-group work might include time limits, task lists, and assigned discussion roles (e.g., notetaker, questioner, scribe, mediator, or publisher). Small-group work encourages teamwork and communication. It also provides a low-stakes environment to practice dialogic interaction, preparing students to go dialogic in whole-class discussion. | Prepare, Practice |
| DRAMA ACTIVITIES<br><br>Collaborative role play or performance. Students can act out a scene from a novel, create a tableau of a significant moment, conduct a choral reading, or interpret the plot of a story in a different setting, for example. | Practice |
| ROLE-PLAYING GAMES<br><br>Collaborative role play or performance. Students take on roles, as in drama activities, but usually with more codified rules and structure. They can participate in talk shows, develop radio call-in shows, or put authors on trial. | Practice |
| *Tools to Position Students to Direct Interaction* | |
| STUDENT-WRITTEN QUESTIONS<br><br>Questions students prepare in advance of a lesson. Students develop and write out questions to generate learning talk. Having students write the questions encourages higher levels of thinking and offers students autonomy and authority. | Prepare |

| | |
|---|---|
| PASS TOY<br><br>An object (a small toy, ball, or stuffed animal) passed from one student to the next, regulating who has the floor. Students choose who has the next turn by throwing the pass toy. | Practice |
| STUDENT TOKEN<br><br>Small objects distributed before a large-group discussion, used as admission to it. If students receive two tokens, for example, they can speak up twice. Using tokens can encourage more students to speak and thwart domination by one or a few vocal students. | Prepare, Practice |
| *Tools to Make Norms and Procedures Explicit* | |
| META-LESSONS<br><br>Lessons explicitly addressing how to participate in classroom talk. You might use meta-lessons to establish expectations, communicate norms, revisit rules, or negotiate standards for the quantity and quality of participation in classroom talk. Meta-lessons vary in the extent to which the teacher defines the norms or invites students to do so. | Prepare, Reflect |
| SENTENCE AND QUESTION STEMS<br><br>A list of words and phrases used to introduce a speaker's message. These stems can scaffold students into civil conversation by providing them with ways of cuing respectful agreement and disagreement and providing them with ideas for questions, for example, "I agree, and I'd also like to add . . . " and "I respectfully disagree, because. . .". | |
| *Tools to Organize Physical Space* | |
| SEATING CONFIGURATION<br><br>Deliberate arrangement of furniture within space. You can arrange classroom space and furniture to allow students to see and hear each other, for example, by putting chairs in a circle or in small groups. Such classroom arrangements can interrupt the expected teacher-student hierarchy and promote student learning talk. You can use small and large circles, carousel, U-shapes, and desks facing each other in clusters of three or four. | Practice |

*You can find examples of the tools throughout the book and on our companion website (vbrr.wiki.educ.msu.edu.)

*Advantages:* Teacher-led tools offer teachers the opportunity to front-load much of the work of generating student talk. For example, you can spend time before a lesson composing thoughtful questions for a Four Corners activity or an anticipation guide, rather than having to improvise questions in the middle of a lesson. Some teacher-led tools also often give students time to prepare. For example, composing prompts give students an opportunity to process their thinking in writing, rather than their having to develop thoughts on the fly. Overall, teacher-led tools can provide teachers with ways to structure ongoing interaction in productive ways.

*Points to Consider:* As a teacher leading discussion, you may use questioning techniques, such as uptake or repetition (see Chapter 2), that may be unfamiliar to students. In the following example, 10th-grade teacher Elnora Greenstein planned that she would maintain responsibility for soliciting and directing the flow of dialogue in ways that would support her central objectives for learning. At the same time, she planned to take less of an authoritative role and encourage students to evaluate their own responses about the use of language in *Great Expectations*. Elnora prompted the class to identify words that contributed to establishing mood:

> JESSE: How about *undistinguishable*?
> TEACHER: All right, so what about *undistinguishable*?
> JESSE: Wow, I just said that and you copied me.
> TEACHER: No, I'm responding to you. But what about it?
> JESSE: The fact that something is so covered in cobwebs, fungus and
>     cobwebs, that you can't recognize it. That's pretty gross.

Students unfamiliar with uptake may not understand why a teacher might repeat what they say. You might consider explaining to students why you are taking the role that you are in classroom talk. Talking to students about techniques like uptake can help reveal some of what's behind the curtain in terms of making good conversation for learning. It can also give students ownership of these techniques for their own use. "A Student Questionnaire," found on our website (vbrr.wiki.educ.msu.edu), can help facilitate meta-talk about classroom talk.

## Student-Led Tools

Student-led tools encourage greater student influence on the direction of classroom dialogue. While both teacher- and student-led tools elicit student voices, student-led tools turn the reins over to students to direct the course of the dialogue. Teachers can use student-led tools to

- Organize students into configurations conducive to their directing of dialogue, for example, arranging the desks into a circle;

- Prepare students with the language they need to direct dialogue, for example, offering students sentence starters for interactive dialogues. For examples of sentence starters, see "How Can I Contribute to Classroom Dialogue?" on our website (vbrr.wiki.educ.msu.edu);
- Scaffold students to direct dialogue, for example, asking students to generate the questions themselves; and
- Offer norms and structures within which students can direct substantive and complex instances of dialogue (e.g., debate, Socratic seminar).

Even as students become more proficient and independent as participants in classroom talk, they still benefit from the scaffolding offered by dialogic tools that help to structure talk.

*Advantages:* Although student-led tools usually involve the teacher's choice of text, topic, and participation structure, they do afford students greater opportunity to take the lead in classroom talk and to produce classroom knowledge. They provide structural support for more student turns and fewer teacher turns. Turn-taking tools, like a soft object thrown from speaker to speaker (a *pass toy*), enable the teacher to step back and allow students some of the responsibility for turn taking. Meta-lessons make the inner workings of classroom interactions more visible and support students as they assume responsibility for smooth and productive dialogue.

*Points to Consider:* Students enter classrooms carrying with them accumulated experiences with typical classroom talk. Some of these experiences may color how they experience your attempts at dialogic teaching. As with teacher-led talk, it becomes important to discover students' expectations and then address how these expectations fit in with your vision for student learning talk.

Students may have their own opinions on the value of student learning talk. For example, Logan Cloe encouraged his high school students to maintain a discussion around the science fiction novel *Feed:*

CHRIS: Dude, the teacher's trying to get out of teaching.
CLASS: [Laughter.]
TEACHER: Oh, man. The ultimate goal of a teacher is to be able to set you up, stand back, and let you just discuss it.
CHRIS: And they get paid to just sit in a chair.

The extensive planning on your part, on display in this chapter, may be part of where you earn your pay, even if this work becomes largely invisible as work per se to students.

Students likely have years of experience in addressing the teacher rather than their peers in class. These familiar routines aren't going to be easily disrupted just because you've set up the expectation that students should be talking to each other.

For example, Caroline Weekley's students were a bit uncertain about how to proceed when she asked them to consider her as "just another participant" and not as a "teacher":

> SAM: Are we asking this to you [looking at teacher] or are we just asking?
> TEACHER: Oh, no, you're just asking. All of you are looking at me and there's a rule on the guideline sheet, "Do not look at your teacher."
> SAM: But you're not a teacher in this whole thing.
> TEACHER: I'm a participant, you're right. So, I will raise my hand if there's a question I have. But y'all must think I'm looking fresh today because you keep looking at me.
> SAM: Nope.
> CLASS: [Laughter.]

As this example illustrates, students may need support and repeated attempts to become comfortable with your expectations for classroom talk. You may also need to build students' trust around these types of interactions. It may be possible that they've had experiences with teachers who explicitly expressed a desire for them to talk to each other but implicitly maintained their positions as central addressee. Establishing new norms can be tough, but visual and verbal cues can make this task easier. For example, you might consider taking a seat in the back of the room, sitting side by side with students in a circle (as Jackie did, discussed in Chapter 2), or offering students the use of a pass toy to manage turn taking. Student-led tools can help teachers avoid default behaviors. In addition to using tools, you might consider sharing your rationale for dialogic interactions to address the spoken and silent misconceptions students may hold.

## TOOLS TO PREPARE, PRACTICE, AND REFLECT

We've categorized the tools in Tables 3.1 and 3.2 according to their functions of prepare, practice, or reflect. To illustrate these categories, let's return to our cooking example. Once you figure out how to zest your lemon, you read the second recipe instruction: "Mix oil, spices, and vinegar and marinate chicken in mixture overnight." And you realize you don't have an "overnight"; your guests are arriving in 3 hours. In dialogic instruction, *prepare* tools do the "mixing and marinating" work ahead of time, while *practice* and *reflect* tools focus on dishing up, savoring, and learning from your efforts.

- *Prepare* tools give both students and teacher the opportunity to brainstorm and organize ideas before being asked to dialogue about ideas, ensuring that no one is caught unprepared like the cook in the dinner party example.

- *Practice* tools support teachers and students as they engage in talking-to-learn. When talking to learn, students draw on preparation, pose and respond to questions, follow rules for collegial learning talk, and define individual roles.
- *Reflect* tools give teachers and students the opportunity to process the ideas they raised and to brainstorm possible revisions to their dialogic practice.

Being aware of these tools is a starting point. But planning for learning talk involves also selecting tools (or even inventing new ones), sequencing them, and supporting their use in classroom practice. Let's follow new teacher Kimberly Longley through these stages in her planning.

## SELECT, SEQUENCE, SUPPORT

### Select and Sequence

Selecting appropriate tools can help you to elicit student voices. Sequencing tools in targeted combination with each other (just like mixing ingredients) can make dialogue with students even more effective. Our research found that teachers who combined multiple tools in a given lesson were more likely to achieve high rates of student participation than were those who used none or only one tool (Caughlan et al., 2013).

Kimberly Longley taught a literature unit around the novel *Frankenstein* in her English 10 class. Unit goals included students having an understanding of themes common to the horror literature and their actively participating in student-led discussions about the novel. (See Chapter 4 for a discussion of sequencing tools over time to achieve these larger goals.)

In past lessons, Kimberly's students had struggled in student-led discussions. Upon reflection, Kimberly realized that she had not done enough to establish expectations or scaffold students' understanding of their roles and responsibilities in the discussion. Based on previous experience, she selected and sequenced tools to support students in preparing, practicing, and reflecting on their experience with a big-idea discussion grounded in the reading of literature. To these ends, she selected and sequenced the following tools: meta-lesson, composing prompt, student-written questions, Socratic seminar/fishbowl, and reflection/self-assessment worksheet. The actual materials Kimberly generated appear in the text boxes.

*Meta-Lesson (Teacher-Led/Prepare):* Kimberly prepared a handout (see below) to outline the norms and expectations for participating in a Socratic seminar. She used the handout to lead a discussion with students. Kimberly chose to make the rules discussion teacher led; however, you may prefer to have students contribute to establishing rules for discussion.

### Inside the Classroom: Kimberly's Handout

*Note: This handout is itself a tool that orients students to the coordinated activities of this lesson, including responding to a writing prompt, engaging in a meta-lesson, and planning for and enacting a Socratic seminar.*

The Socratic Method (or Method of Elenchus or Socratic Debate) is a form of inquiry and debate between individuals with opposing viewpoints based on asking and answering questions to stimulate rational thinking and to illuminate ideas. —Wikipedia.com

In order to begin thinking critically about the implications of the themes from *Frankenstein*, we will be having a Socratic seminar during which you will discuss your attitudes and perspectives pertaining to some of the themes. To clarify, a Socratic seminar entails a discussion of a preselected topic for which there is no clear-cut "right" or "wrong" answer. The purpose of this sort of discussion is to listen and respond to various viewpoints with the goal of reaching a deeper level of understanding.

The topic for the seminar is as follows: "In what ways do human beings 'play God' every day? What are the pros and cons?"

\*\*\*

In order to be an active and engaged member of a Socratic seminar, one must be prepared. Preparation entails having kept up with the reading of the novel, marking/noting appropriate passages from the text that support or refute your arguments, thinking critically and thoughtfully about the questions before the discussion, and being prepared to relate many major thoughts back to the text. Bring all prep materials (the novel, notes, questions, etc.) with you to the seminar. Students who come unprepared to a Socratic seminar bring down the rest of the group and can provide a distraction. Therefore, unprepared students will not be allowed to participate and will forfeit their grade. Evidence of preparation must be shown to a teacher before a student is allowed to participate.

### *RULES*

Socratic seminars often bring about authentic, charged-up debates. In fact, this is one of their purposes! However, rules ensure order as well as a respectful, comfortable environment.

1.  *One speaker at a time.* It is not necessary to raise your hand, but once someone is speaking, it is expected that every other member is politely listening. If many people want to step in at once, the facilitator will mediate.
2.  *No "conversation hogs."* Participation is expected, but participation in a seminar also means allowing full involvement by all in the discussion. "Hogs" will be penalized.
3.  *Be polite.* Disagreements may (and often do) arise. However, politely disagreeing is key and expected. Raising your voice, pointing fingers, swearing, and so on will result in a 0 for the discussion. If you wouldn't say it in class normally, don't say it in the seminar.
4.  *Stay on topic.* The facilitator will step in if conversation veers drastically off course. It should go without saying that side conversations (meaning any that don't pertain directly to the discussion at hand) will result in the student leaving the discussion and forfeiting his or her grade.

**Violation of any of the rules will result in a loss of points (and possible removal from the discussion).**

**Inside the Classroom: Kimberly's Handout 2**

*Socratic Seminar Reflection*

*Opening Question(s):* In what ways do human beings "play God" every day? What are the pros and cons?

1.  Summary of key ideas: _____
2.  Reaction: Identify one idea or statement that was made during the seminar that struck you. Write a brief (1–3 sentences) reaction to that idea.
3.  Explain how the seminar influenced your thinking about the topic or the text(s).

Self-Assessment

| | | | | | |
|---|---|---|---|---|---|
| Taking a position on a question | 5 | 4 | 3 | 2 | 1 |
| Using evidence to support a position or presenting factual information | 5 | 4 | 3 | 2 | 1 |
| Drawing another person into the discussion | 5 | 4 | 3 | 2 | 1 |
| Asking a clarifying question or moving the discussion along | 5 | 4 | 3 | 2 | 1 |
| Highlighting and marking the text with questions/commentary | 5 | 4 | 3 | 2 | 1 |

*Composing Prompt and Student-Written Questions (Teacher- and Student-Led/Prepare):* For homework, Kimberly asked students to make notes, mark passages, and raise questions related to one big-idea question, "In what ways do human beings 'play God' every day? What are the pros and cons?"

*Socratic Seminar Fishbowl (Student-Led/Practice):* Students talked about the big-idea question. For organizational purposes—and to make sure students could get a word in—Kimberly split the class into two groups, or two concentric circles. While the inner circle of students participated in the discussion, the outer-circle students took notes on ideas raised and patterns of participation. Then the groups switched. Kimberly planned for each group to have 20 minutes to talk, with 2 minutes of transition time. In her lesson plan, she noted that she "(will) speak very little, but will take notes for assessment purposes, will reroute if issues get off topic, or will step in if discussion gets decidedly heated or inappropriate."

*Reflection/Self-Assessment Worksheet (Teacher- and Student-Led/Reflect):* Kimberly asked her students to reflect on the Socratic seminar. She provided two different ways to do this reflection:

- A qualitative measure (words); and
- A quantitative measure (scale rankings).

Such reflections may serve multiple purposes, such as improving quality of talk for next time, affirming good things that happened that day, and providing a space for students to capture in their own words the ideas tossed around. These words may ultimately form the basis for an individual essay or other synthesizing activity.

Kimberly selected a combination of teacher-led tools and student-led tools to meet her desired learning objectives. She sequenced each of these in logical order, using teacher-led tools to prepare students to take responsibility for directing the course of dialogue on their own, and then giving students the opportunity to individually reflect on a whole-group experience.

Kimberly's example illustrates one potential way to select and sequence tools. But you can use many possible ways to sequence tools for student engagement in dialogue. Here is another potentially effective pattern:

1. *Student-to-text.* Have students write a journal entry, work on a pre-discussion worksheet, or share initial ideas in an online discussion forum in response to prompts about the content area.
2. *Student-to-one-other-student.* Invite students to pair up and share some of what they've already written with one other peer.
3. *Student-to-small-group.* Organize small groups of three to four students. Have each partner in a pair describe the ideas of his original partner to the new pair, with each student taking a turn.
4. *Student-to-large-group.* Select another dialogic tool to organize a whole-group discussion of the big ideas.
5. *Student-to-text.* Offer students an opportunity to reflect on the talk of the day in relation to the content area and their changed understanding of it.

## Support Success

It's not just the use of tools that creates conditions for dialogue to flourish; detailed planning in and around the use of these tools is also crucial.

*Behind the Scenes.* Let's look at some of the work Kimberly included in her lesson plan to prepare for and manage the Socratic seminar.

Kimberly thought through the mobilization of her tools from minute to minute within the classroom. She set up the chairs in circles before the students came in, so that class time was not used in moving furniture. As she checked students' prep work, she had three activities occurring simultaneously; neither students nor teacher had idle time. Finally, she had multiple supports to keep rules and expectations available to students: Each student had a copy of the rules: The rules were up on the whiteboard, and Kimberly verbally recapped the expectations.

Clearly, using several tools can mean a lot of moving parts (literally and figuratively). Of course, writing out the details of a lesson as you plan may eventually

**Socratic Seminar**

1. The desks will be set up in circles.
2. Students will begin by taking out the preparation work they should have completed for homework the previous night. I will come around and check that students are prepared; those who are not will not participate in the discussions.
3. As I check prep work, students will draw from a basket of papers with the numbers 1 and 2 on them to determine their fishbowl group.
4. As this occurs, students can complete some last-minute preparation. Unprepared students can still earn minimal points for their note-taking of the discussion.
5. After checking students' prep work, I will spend 5–10 minutes reviewing the format for the discussion and answering any last-minute questions. Reminders/rules will be on the whiteboard for students to refer to.

be unnecessary as you become more and more comfortable with planning and facilitating classroom interactions. However, when you try something new (like dialogic practices), detailed planning can be invaluable.

*Thinking through classroom transitions.* Taking time to think through and teach typical classroom routines can help you minimize potential classroom management challenges as you go dialogic. Some questions to consider include:

- What procedures are in place for moving desks?
- What procedures are in place for returning students from working in small groups to paying attention to the large group?
- How can I make use of visual aids? For each role assigned in a small group, should I create a hat or some other outward sign of the role?
- How can I make use of auditory aids? Should I use a special clap to regain attention and invite students to cease side conversations?
- How can I make use of spatial aids? Should I put tape down on the floor so if desks get moved, they can get moved back into original positions? If I ask students to add notes to a wall, have I made clear how I expect the flow of traffic to move toward and away from the wall?

And all this preparation work? When it culminates in a discussion like Kimberly's students had, the reward is highly engaged student learning talk.

*How Dialogic Tools Can Culminate in Student Learning Talk.* Kimberly set out to teach her students to independently navigate norms for participating in discussion. She wanted them to prepare for discussion so they could contribute their own perspectives with evidence. She also wanted them to listen carefully to others' divergent perspectives and consider a complex topic in nuanced ways. She further wanted their discussion about a real-world topic to expand their thinking about the novel they had read and vice versa. And what about the standards? If you recall from Chapter 1, the CCSS includes goals for participating in discussion, for example "to prepare for and participate effectively in a range of conversations and collaborations with diverse partners, building on others' ideas and expressing their own clearly and persuasively; to respond thoughtfully to diverse perspectives; to resolve contradictions when possible" (CCSS Initiative, 2010, p. 48). Although the CCSS were not yet developed when Kimberly taught this course, her dialogic approach—and her unit goal for student participation in discussion—aligns clearly with learning goals articulated in the CCSS.

Having looked closely at Kimberly's planning process and reviewed her goals, let's take a closer look at how students responded. Here's part of a transcript from students who participated in the Socratic seminar:

JANA: We're always trying to attempt to prolong human life, I guess, after it should. I'm not saying that we should die when we get hurt, or like when we get sick, but we definitely try to prolong it past the point that where it should be prolonged. For instance, like, the people that are in comas on life support and whatnot . . .

PAT: Umm, like sometimes medicine, isn't good, like it can make them live longer which can make them, like, struggle or be in pain when like, if they were to die they'd be at peace, and on page 85, umm, it says, "I wish sometimes to shake off all the thought of feeling, but I learned that there was but one means to overcome the sensation of pain, and that was death," so it's kind of like, if the medicine is keeping you alive then you'll be in pain longer than if you were to just not have medicine.

TYLER: Umm, I really think, kind of getting to the con part of umm, trying to play God and like, people trying to attempt to live longer through surgeries and medicines and whatever, umm, it kind of prevents natural selection and, um, like, the strongest will survive and stuff like that. And then also, like Milly gave an example one day in class about, um, people can predetermine genders, uh, for the babies and that kind of prevents, umm, genetic variability and that thing, and that could end up wiping out the entire human race because, umm, because we're not allowing that to happen and so everyone can catch the same disease and all that.

ALEX: Exactly. It's really scary to think about the fact that one day, every single person in the world will be the exact same and then one bad thing could kill everybody.

JADEN: [Low.] That seems highly unlikely.

ALEX: What?

JADEN: I said that seems highly unlikely that everyone would be exactly the same.

ALEX: What? I mean if we use the same means to create every life and then it wouldn't be varied in any sense, right? I guess . . . but I'm not saying to the extreme . . . then that would be the case.

PAT: What do you guys think about like, umm, I'm not sure if I'm—can even talk about it . . . but like, assisted suicide at all? Like some doctors, umm, helping, like if the pain is too much for some patients, that they give them morphine and [inaudible] help them kill themselves, and so they can umm . . .

XAVIER: I think it kind of like depends, I guess, on religion, because, I mean it's against the law to kill yourself, but, um, I think kind of like with the abortion thing, like it's your own body, it's your own decision. If you want to be in the world, you can and if you don't want to, it should be your decision. I'm not saying everybody should go kill themselves but, like, doctors shouldn't . . . doctors shouldn't be allowed to help but they should be allowed to stop treatment based on the person and not, like, their family.

Pat's comment reveals that he came to the discussion prepared, having read and researched material under study. He explicitly drew on that preparation by referring to evidence from texts and other research on the topic or issue to stimulate a thoughtful, well-reasoned exchange of ideas. In his subsequent comment, Tyler drew upon Milly's dialogue from a previous day and paraphrased her contribution to make connections across class sessions.

As the discussion continued, Jaden challenged Alex, but Alex did not attack him in his response; rather he responded in a civil way that sustained the line of reasoning. Pat then posed a new question to the whole group about assisted suicide. Both he and Xavier responded thoughtfully to diverse perspectives, summarized points of agreement and disagreement, and, when warranted, qualified or justified their own views and understanding. They also made new connections in light of the evidence and reasoning presented.

By carefully sequencing dialogic tools, Kimberly supported students in assuming more and more responsibility for discussion. She offered them an opportunity to practice with norms and rules for collegial discussions and decision making (e.g., informal consensus, presentation of alternate views). And she provided a learning opportunity in which students were able to explore their thoughts on a complex real-world issue in ways that supported their construction of their own interpretations of the novel they studied.

Kimberly and her class did not hold this Socratic seminar on the first day of class, or even during their first unit. This achievement built upon Kimberly's expectations that students engage in learning talk and on previous lessons that built students' capacities to hold independent discussions. The next chapter examines in more depth how dialogic classrooms are built over time.

CHAPTER 4

# Planning for the Long Haul

If planning for a lesson is like preparing for a meal, then planning for the semester or year is like considering your diet over the long term. You make sure you have all the nutrients you need to grow strong and stay healthy, while keeping taste, color, and variety in mind to motivate yourself to eat well. As you move through the semester or year, how can you offer students a nourishing and sustaining diet of classroom talk? At first, just getting more students to come to the table and engage in academic conversation may seem like a major hurdle, but then you may want to encourage their generative questioning and engagement with the text, concepts, and each other. This process involves sequencing the interactional skills you intend to teach over time. Planning for dialogic talk within a unit involves strategic thinking about what participation structures you use, when you use them, and how you use them to both build on what students have done before and prepare them for what is to come. This chapter provides you with ways to plan for dialogic instruction over the longer term of a unit, a semester, or a year.

This chapter also introduces the idea that dialogic teaching is not just about your approach to structuring interactions among the individuals in the classroom; taking a dialogic stance affects how you approach designing units, implementing standards, articulating goals, and creating assignments at the curricular level.

## PLANNING FOR THE LONG HAUL

Chapter 1 introduced the concept of *cumulation* (Alexander, 2008; Mercer, 2000): Talking to learn becomes cumulative when teachers and students build on contributions and ideas over time. Cumulative talk can be seen within individual lessons as the teacher and students respond to each other's comments and make connections among them. However, cumulation goes beyond the individual conversation to draw attention to the ways in which *curriculum* can be dialogic (Applebee, 1996). Considering curricular coherence involves thinking

## A Teacher Reflects: Melinda

Melinda Vallarta reflected on her late November lesson on *The Canterbury Tales*, where her students had discussed the proverb "The love of money is the root of all evil," featured in "The Pardoner's Tale." She felt that she and her students had progressed since an earlier videotaped lesson, where her focus had been on increasing her use of authentic questions ("baby steps toward discussion"). Some aspects of the conversation pleased her:

> I felt as if I had a much better mix of responses. This can be directly attributed to the fact that I had a greater variety of students who volunteered. I think the pre-writing activity definitely contributed to this. The students felt more comfortable because they had the extra time to organize and compose their thoughts in the journal before sharing with the class. I also was impressed by the uptake that I saw. I know I need to encourage this more often, but it was a start. I feel that their conversation is more valuable when they are responding to each other and not to me.

At the same time, however, she also noticed too many side conversations and too many students still directing their contributions back to her rather than to each other.

Melinda indicated her intentions for future lessons: working herself out of the conversation so that students would respond to each other directly; asking students to support their claims with textual support (missing in the first two conversations); and rearranging the classroom so the desks were not in rows. Achieving these goals would also require meta-lessons on politeness norms and productive discussion protocols. Students had sabotaged an early attempt at whole-class discussion in a circle by engaging in coordinated pencil tapping—she had since backed off rearranging the seats until she could figure out how to make it work.

Melinda understood that apprenticing her opinionated students into productive academic discussions would not occur overnight. Not only did she recognize that they lacked experience with such learning talk; she also recognized her own tendency to mediate every exchange:

> I think my most ambitious goal will be extracting myself so the students are talking to one another and not going through me. Although I don't consider myself a control freak, I am afraid to do this because my mentor and I have frequently discussed how easily this particular class will go off on tangents.

Going dialogic in this classroom involved an ambitious combination of coordinating academic expectations, student and teacher behaviors, and the physical setup of the classroom.

about the design of curriculum on a larger scale. If you conceptualize "curriculum as conversation" (Applebee, 1996), then you want your students to enter the culturally significant traditions of English language arts through their engagement with texts, teachers, and each other. Within curriculum, texts are in conversation with each other, ideas are in conversation, and both texts and ideas are in conversation with real-world concerns. For example, all the texts studied in a semester might build on the theme of "investigating social worlds" (Beach & Myers, 2001), and the writing assignments might call on students to compare and contrast how authors approach the theme, tell narratives set within their own social worlds, or compare their own social worlds with those of texts.

In other words, taking a dialogic stance toward curriculum means more than just choosing texts and assignments: It also involves taking a dialogic stance on curriculum planning at the year, semester, or unit level. The idea of teaching according to dialogic principles is more consistent with certain stances on the discipline of English than others. For example, teachers who give multiple choice textbook tests promoting single interpretations of literary texts as their major assessment of student learning will probably prefer to maintain control of topic, turn taking, and interpretation, because they see themselves possessing the single interpretation that needs to be deposited into students (Freire, 1970). Within such a framework, it makes sense that students might resist invitations to engage in open discussion. In their experience the teacher has all the answers that count!

In contrast, creating coherence means planning for dialogic teaching on all levels. Dialogic teachers design encounters with texts and with ideas that put students in conversation with the living traditions of reading and responding to literature, and communicating through talk and writing. They do not build walls between the reading, writing, thinking, and listening elements of the English language arts but build connections among them. As a dialogic teacher, you might do the following:

- Refer to what a student said in a conversation the week before in making a point.
- Have the same small groups meet throughout a semester to conduct a shared inquiry into a community issue, and present their results to the community at the end of the semester (Duke, Caughlan, Juzwik, & Martin, 2012). As students work together, you might begin by tightly structuring student activities, perhaps by assigning roles and keeping strict time limits, but gradually give students more responsibility for carrying out their investigations and conversations.
- Offer students several choices of novels related to the unit theme, so that classroom conversations call on a variety of perspectives on an idea.

## CREATING CURRICULAR COHERENCE

## Planning for Dialogic Teaching with State or National Standards

Now let's shift the focus to applying a dialogic stance toward standards. Remember: Standards set goals of knowledge and skills for students to master within larger units of time, but they do not dictate the means by which students will get there. As we pointed out in Chapter 1, teachers are "informed professionals" (Luke, Woods, & Weir, 2013) who draw on standards as just one element to articulate and achieve academic and developmental goals for their students.

*Some Background.* In general, standards have addressed the idea of talking to learn inconsistently. In the United States, the English language arts content standards developed by most states in the 1990s and 2000s included speaking and listening standards. While in some states these standards were largely confined to public speaking and making presentations (for example, see Florida's 2008 standards at etc.usf.edu/flstandards/la/crosswalk/communication-9-12.pdf), other states also included standards for contributing to small- and large-group discussions. Unfortunately, most states did not assess talking and listening skills using standardized measures, so many teachers felt they could not afford the time to have students engage in dialogic conversations when so much other content would be tested. As a result, talking to learn gave way to more direct instruction. Ironically enough, the research conducted during this time (discussed in Part I), by linking dialogic practices such as authentic questions and open discussion to higher student achievement, strengthened the case for dialogic instruction even while teachers struggled to put students' voices at the core of their curriculum.

As of this writing, the consortia responsible for writing tests for states adopting the Common Core State Standards (CCSS) are considering developing standardized speaking and listening tests, but we still do not know whether these items will make it into the final version of state exams. However, the CCSS provide examples of how standards can offer openings for dialogic instruction in two ways: by including speaking and listening standards that emphasize discussion and by including reading and writing standards that can be better met by incorporating dialogic interaction into classrooms.

*Speaking and Listening Standards.* The CCSS provide six standards for speaking and listening: three for comprehension and collaboration, and three for presentation of knowledge and ideas (referring to more formal presentations of speech and media). The comprehension and collaboration anchor standards refer specifically to skills related to the types of "speaking out" and "taking in" introduced in Chapter 2:

1. Prepare for and participate effectively in a range of conversations and collaborations with diverse partners, building on others' ideas and expressing their own clearly and persuasively.
2. Integrate and evaluate information presented in diverse media and formats, including visually, quantitatively, and orally.
3. Evaluate a speaker's point of view, reasoning, and use of evidence and rhetoric (CCSS Initiative, 2010, p. 48).

The grade 11–12 standards for participating in conversations and collaborations set a high bar for student autonomy, for example: "Respond thoughtfully to diverse perspectives; synthesize comments, claims, and evidence made on all sides of an issue; resolve contradictions when possible; and determine what additional information or research is required to deepen the investigation or complete the task" (CCSS Initiative, Speaking and Listening Standard 1d, p. 50). Carefully sequencing dialogic tools (particularly meta-lessons and other student-led tools) can enable students to work with peers to evaluate ideas and perspectives and to develop arguments. With support, students can develop judgment and autonomy.

*Writing and Reading Standards.* The CCSS writing and reading standards, like those for speaking and listening, emphasize responding to different perspectives and considering and resolving divergent views. Students at the middle and high school levels should read across texts, make connections, and use evidence to support a proposition in reading both literary and informational texts—a very dialogic orientation. The writing standards provide similar openings for students and teachers to take a dialogic stance. Written argumentation is the major emphasis of the Common Core and an especially important curricular area for dialogic practice. Research supports using discussion and other forms of dialogic teaching in developing arguments (e.g., Murphy et al., 2009; Reznitskaya et al., 2001). Students can develop argument writing skills when they

- Work together to consider evidence;
- Build cases for a claim in pairs or small groups; or
- Deliberate about a question in debate, Socratic seminar, or drama activity.

Chapter 5 discusses argument writing instruction in greater depth.

## Exceeding State Content Standards

Long-term goals can also exceed the minimal learning goals established by the standards to include democratic participation and exploration of moral questions and dilemmas. As we mentioned in Chapter 1, dialogic teaching also plays a critical role in preparing students for civic participation. Melinda Vallarta's goals for the year included promoting civil speech and attentive listening, skills that her diverse students would need for active citizenship. In addition, English teachers have long used literature and writing to have students reflect on values and on the moral consequences of human thoughts and actions (Caughlan, 2011; Juzwik, 2013). While state standards rarely acknowledge such goals explicitly, values and morality frequently appear in talk about literature and narrative writing.

## SEQUENCING TOOLS OVER THE SEMESTER OR THE YEAR

As you approach course design at the beginning of a semester or a year, you can build toward your curricular goals for dialogic interaction among students or among students and texts, authors, and ideas. Moving toward ever more cumulative talk and coherent curriculum involves sequencing activities over time that will teach students how to take on more responsibility for interaction across the semester.

Consider the concept introduced in Part I, "What I say responds to what you said." Achieving this kind of responsive classroom talk requires openings for students to make substantive contributions—to "say" things, for other students to listen and really hear what is said, and for teachers and students both to respond thoughtfully and build on what was said. This dialogic stance takes time and practice. The dialogic tools introduced in Chapter 3 provide the foundation for the planning framework we present in this chapter. Over time, they will facilitate changes in teacher role, student role, classroom environment, and assessment.

The following framework (Table 4.1), also available as a reproducible on the companion website (vbrr.wiki.educ.msu.edu), shows one possible map for moving yourself, your students, the classroom environment, and assessment in more dialogic directions. We recognize that not everyone works on quarterly schedules and not every group will be ready to accept the changes in stance and procedure depicted here at the same time. However, Table 4.1 represents a gradual release of responsibility for directing classroom talk away from teacher-only to shared responsibility with students. The use of tools also evolves, as both teacher and students become adept at using ever more complex tools and navigating a variety of interactional landscapes.

Consider some of the examples you have already read about in light of this proposed journey through a year. Melinda, for example, mainly used open-ended teacher questions in recitation to elicit students' ideas in early October. By the time the lesson described at the start of this chapter occurred, a month and a half later, she was using journal prompts to allow students to develop ideas before conversation. She found that this tool allowed for more well-developed responses on the part of students, both to her prompts and to each other's ideas. By mid-March, students were using a turn-taking tool to manage their student-led discussion of a journal prompt, and Melissa could finally step back, becoming another participant in the conversation.

**Table 4.1. Framework for Sequencing Dialogic Tools over Time**

| | 1st quarter | 2nd quarter | 3rd quarter | 4th quarter |
|---|---|---|---|---|
| Teacher role | T relies on T-L tools in establishing routines and scaffolding students into participation. T may introduce meta-lessons. | While T-L tools continue as a staple of planning, meta-lessons provide a chance to consider alternate roles for Ss and T to try. More structured S-L tools (drama activities, student-written questions) are introduced as needed. | Structured S-L tools (Socratic seminars, student-written questions) become more frequently used. However, T sequences and combines T-L and S-L activities, depending on position within unit. | T designs lessons that expertly combine tools according to the goals of the lesson, unit, or year. T can step back from managing each interaction and rely on established routines as well as invent new ones with Ss. |
| Student role | By taking an active role in classroom activities, students voice their perspectives and become used to taking a role in classroom talk. | Ss continue to engage in T-L activities but may also contribute to the establishment of norms and begin more independent work in small groups. | Ss learn to articulate the purposes for different forms of interaction in the classroom. By using S-L tools, they take more ownership of knowledge production in class. | Ss routinely engage in knowledge production and choice in final projects and activities. |

|  | 1st quarter | 2nd quarter | 3rd quarter | 4th quarter |
|---|---|---|---|---|
| *Classroom environment* | Careful attention to seating charts and arrangement of desks enables productive interaction and curbs unproductive side talk. T instructs Ss in location and use of textual and technological resources. | Ss become used to a changing seating arrangement, depending on the demands of the activity. Ss are aware of available resources and rules for their responsible use. | Classroom is becoming a flexible resource for grouping and participation. Ss can quickly set up different seating arrangements. T abdicates some control of textual and technological resources. | Ss and T see classroom as a flexible resource for grouping and participation. Ss can quickly set up different seating arrangements, and have full access to textual and technological resources. |
| *Assessment* | Classroom talk provides a means of pre-assessment of both content and interactional skills and a means for informal formative assessment. | In addition to oral formative assessment, writing done to prepare for or in response to classroom talk, or composed in pairs or small groups can provide indications of student learning. | Working together, T and Ss develop rubrics for assessing productive academic interaction, such as discussion. Ss thus hold themselves and are held accountable for classroom talk. | Classroom interaction is a major means of creating written works to be assessed and of negotiation over choices for assessment. |

*Key:* Ss=Students; T=Teacher; T-L=Teacher=Led; S-L=Student-Led

Not only can you scaffold increasingly student-led forms of talk over the year, you can also guide students to go into greater depth with the content of that talk. For example, Melinda's early attempts involved students making personal connections to characters in the *Iliad*. During the March student-led discussion of *Hamlet*, however, students "upped the ante" (Adler & Rougle, 2005) by interweaving their stances on mental health issues with specific examples from the text to support their conclusions regarding Hamlet's sanity. The next section shows how you can mobilize dialogic tools to assist in the sort of growth in interactional skills and in digging into content that Melinda's students showed over time.

## Using Teacher-Led Tools to Scaffold Dialogic Interaction

Teacher-led tools are particularly useful early in the semester, to scaffold students into dialogic participation. You can also use them early in a unit to introduce concepts and routines. Consider Melinda's use of a composing prompt early in the process of teaching her students to participate productively. Students wrote on an open-ended prompt related to "The Pardoner's Tale" and then shared their responses to develop a multifaceted interpretation of a short text:

> ELLEN: When I was reading this quote, I think money isn't actually the cause of evil, it's like an effect.
> TEACHER: Oh, okay. So the person is evil inherently and that's what causes them to want money.
> TYRONE: Yeah.
> TEACHER: I never thought about it that way.
> ELLEN: And then I think there's actually not just one cause for evil. Like maybe for each person there's one evil for them, but as a whole there's not just one.

Melinda's students were learning to dig into a short text and respond with their own ideas. Later in the year, students can select the quotes or questions they feel are significant for a given text. Meta-lessons can help transition from teacher-led to student-led tools, because they explicitly address what is involved in productive disciplinary conversations.

## Tools for Establishing Norms and Expectations: Meta-Lessons

Krista Delafuente's students had completed their journal entry for the day: "Tell me about a time you had a good conversation. Why was it good? What makes a conversation good?"

> TEACHER: All right, what makes a good conversation? Who can throw out some ideas? You don't have to read from your journal. Tell me what you guys put. What makes a good conversation? Yes, ma'am.

TAMEKA: When you talk about something that the other person likes.

TEACHER: Okay, so something interesting. All right, what else do we have? Yes, Selena?

SELENA: When you have like, um, a conversation and it's not anything and one person keeps on talking for a long time.

TEACHER: Okay, so when, wait, okay. So when one person keeps talking and the other person's not really listening?

SELENA: I mean like both of them at the same time trying to keep talking to each other.

TEACHER: Okay, so you have people listening and talking. All right, what else do we got? What else makes a good conversation? What kind of listening do we need? The kind that's not happening right now. What kind of listening do we need?

MARCIE: Oh . . . both sides need to be listening.

TEACHER: All right, so let's talk about this. For discussion in here, let's say I come up with a really interesting topic. But what do you guys need to do before you come to class, in order to talk about this interesting topic?

This talk is more than idle conversation about conversation. It is a meta-lesson about the kinds of discussions Krista and her students want to have in their classroom. It also marks a step forward in students' working understanding of what constitutes productive learning talk: In her final comment, Krista redirects the responses about everyday conversations toward a consideration of academic discussion.

Krista taught this lesson to her pre–advanced placement (AP) 9th-grade English students in an urban school. She had struggled with her beginning efforts at dialogic instruction: "I have a hard time keeping their attention and getting them to talk during our class sessions. I'm not sure if this is because they are freshmen and haven't had practice with discussion or if it's all things I need to do better." Like Melinda Vallarta, however, she knew that dialogic interaction did not happen spontaneously and that she would have to use a variety of tools over time to achieve her goals.

Meta-lessons occupy a unique place among student-led tools. Because teachers and students engaged in meta-lessons pause to explicitly consider how talking-to-learn comes about, and to consider procedures to make it safe and productive, meta-lessons provide a good foundation for developing norms and expectations, a necessary step as students take on more responsibility for classroom talk and knowledge production. You can handle these conversations about conversation in different ways. Some teachers draw on their experience to develop rules for discussion that they use from year to year, so that they are just part of the classroom expectations students learn at the beginning of the semester. Others, like Krista, write the expectations for discussion *with* their students. This choice gives the students a voice in setting norms—and norms are, by definition, developed by and for a group. It can also help students link academic conversation to types of interaction they already know, thus valuing out-of-school ways of talking. Several teachers in our study found their expectations and rules for participation shifting as students became more adept at dialogic interaction.

At the end of this conversation, Krista drew up a list of guidelines for discussion that grew out of students' suggestions and her own goals for classroom interaction. This list was similar to Kimberly Longley's list in Chapter 3. We wish we could say that students enthusiastically put those guidelines into use immediately and quickly became dialogic superstars. However, teaching is usually more complicated than that. Over time, Krista continued to build on her attempts to get more than a few students to contribute to a discussion and to diminish distracting side conversations (learn more about how to deal with that issue in the Coda). By the end of the school year, she noted that although she saw room for growth, the combination of setting rules with her students and holding discussions in a circle resulted in students' respecting each other more, and created more of a community. Students also noted the difference: "It was not really led by the teacher, but it's like everybody in a circle talks to one another, gets along with one another. And we communicate with each other more."

## Using Meta-Lessons to Transition to Student-Led Tools

Krista's meta-lesson took place in early October, after she had had time to get to know her students but early in their journey toward dialogic interaction. She planned the lesson for that day carefully, using many of the ideas for sequencing introduced in Chapter 3. The journal prompt on good conversations led into the meta-lesson and was immediately followed by a practice discussion of Gary Soto's poem "Oranges," using the Wonder Question technique, with which students read and mark up a short text and then write "I wonder . . . " questions (Adler & Rougle, 2005, pp. 48–49). She collected students' questions in a bowl to pick at random, so that students' ideas drove the discussion without putting anyone on the spot. She ended the lesson with a quick wrap-up, debriefing how they liked the poem and how the discussion format had worked.

Note the similarities between this lesson and Kimberley Longley's sequencing of dialogic tools in Chapter 3. Krista's sequence began with a teacher-led tool (a journal entry composing prompt) that continued with the meta-lesson built around that journal entry and was followed by the student-led strategy of having students write their own questions for the poem under discussion. Krista used the questions anonymously for this first trial of student-written questions, in order to give students a more sheltered experience of hearing their questions used as a tool to move the interpretation of the poem forward.

## A Closer Look: Varieties of Student-Written Questions

Chapter 2 provided a short list of question types associated with talking-to-learn, rather than talking to display known correct answers. Student questions are particularly important in learning talk. The way you introduce this tool, the sorts of questions you have students write, and the deployment of the questions in class interaction can all vary, depending on your purposes. In addition to the Wonder Question technique described above, other approaches can help students compose questions that spark learning talk:

- Teach students to ask (and answer) four types of questions depending on where one finds the answer: Right There (in the text), Pulling It Together, Text and Me, and On My Own (Raphael, Highfield, & Au, 2006).
- Use the Dense Question Strategy by teaching students to develop different types of questions related to the text, the reader's knowledge, and the world (Christenbury & Kelly, 1983). Questions develop "density" by combining these sources of knowledge.
- Have students prepare questions in advance of a Socratic seminar, as shown in Chapter 3, grounded in close reading of texts.
- Teach students to compose questions in advance of student-led literary discussions. Show them how to compose open-ended questions that address various aspects of the reading: inferences, effects of literary technique, generalizations to society at large, and so on (Smagorinsky, 2002).

## Student-Led Tools: Deepening the Dialogic Conversation over Time

Over time, you can make use of more student-led tools as students gain expertise in dialogic interaction. As discussed in Chapter 3, you can use some of the student-led tools to physically reorient your classroom in ways that help you share control with your students. Putting chairs in a circle, with you as one participant, is a beginning. Grouping desks so that the students face each other also signals to students that they do important work together. If you use a pass toy during whole-class discussion (see Table 4.1), then you are only one possible holder of the object. Over time, you build a repertoire of signals that dialogic interaction is expected.

We consider student-enacted tools a special kind of student-led tool. Your job is to scaffold participation by creating a structure that requires student participation and leadership to make it work. For example, consider Kimberley Longley's Socratic seminar in Chapter 3. The actual student-led conversation about *Frankenstein* was embedded in an activity structure that included tools to prepare (meta-lesson, composing prompt), participate (the spatial tool of concentric fish-bowl circles, the seminar rules for sticking to the text), and reflect (the reflective writing assignment after the discussion). The teacher took the lead in setting up the activity, but the students actually implemented it. As time goes on and students gain experience in asking questions and proposing ideas, this scaffolding becomes less important. Toward the end of the year, student-enacted tools still signal to students that their participation will take a certain shape and direction on occasion, but as dialogic interactions become more routine special structures may not always be necessary.

## PLANNING FOR ASSESSMENT OVER THE YEAR

Assessment of dialogic instruction can take at least three directions:

1. Using student talk as formative assessment: You gain information about what students understand and what their misconceptions are from what they say.
2. Assessing students' performance in classroom talk (this is less common and more controversial).
3. Assessing your own progress as a dialogic teacher. If you develop and use methods of tracking student engagement in discussion, and means for analyzing qualities of talk, you can use them to assess your own practice.

You can also consider assessment for any of these purposes by recognizing the different ways to gather evidence of student learning in the context of dialogic teaching:

- Collect materials students produce to prepare for dialogic interaction (e.g., journal entries, anticipation guide sheets).
- Evaluate classroom interaction as it occurs, through the use of such tools as maps, checklists, rubrics, and observation notes.
- Collect products of classroom talk (e.g., small-group projects, reflections on a discussion, essays citing what was said in discussion).

### Classroom Talk as Formative Assessment

What students say in the classroom is one indication of what they think. You can ask questions related to the core understandings of a lesson or a unit at intervals, or at the end of a lesson, and see how students respond. Indeed a major purpose of recitation is to check for understanding. Student questions also provide important information in this vein. Yet even when using classroom talk as assessment in a dialogic classroom, the problem with this method is that you only really know what those who responded to your questions think, and the rest of the group might not share that understanding. To get a sense of what the whole class thinks, consider collecting a brief written assignment, such as a 1-minute paper checking for main takeaway point and lingering questions (Angelo & Cross, 1993). If you want to do a check of students' developing skills in substantive talk, record a class section and study individual exchanges for evidence of how students respond to the text and to each other. We model this process of assessment throughout the book, and Chapter 6 provides instruction on how to study your own classroom using recordings and transcripts.

## Assessing Individual Achievement of Dialogic Interaction

Teachers' internal conflicts abound as they try to develop a collaborative classroom climate while still working within an educational system based on grading and ranking individuals. Such a grading and ranking climate results in the devaluing of anything not assigned a grade. The traditional wisdom is that teachers evaluate thinking when students put it on paper. They create assignments and rubrics where students know that if they meet the mark, they will receive a grade that acknowledges their achievement. The upside of evaluation is that it offers students, parents, and teachers a means of observing progress over time. Unfortunately, a focus on grading makes many teachers and students reluctant to spend time in ungraded learning talk. In such a climate, it can be difficult to find the language for explaining to administrators how students are progressing in course goals through the use of student learning talk. To address this concern, teachers and researchers have developed ways to assess and grade individual achievement in classroom talk (Harris, 1996; Hess & Posselt, 2002; Matanzo, 1996). Kimberly Longley, for example, developed just such a rubric for student self-assessment of participation and preparation as she planned her *Frankenstein* unit (see Figure 4.1).

We see positive and negative aspects of this endeavor. On the positive side, tracking and grading substantive participation in classroom talk establishes its importance. The act of creating rubrics, checklists, and other tools used to describe and rank student talk behaviors provides an opportunity for meta-lessons about the goals of talk-based activity, and the types of behaviors to strive toward. For example, Kimberly's rubric directed students' attention to an expectation that they make explicit references to texts in the Socratic seminar. Such tools will vary according to the goals of a particular activity, and teachers can design them to focus students' activity in particular substantive or procedural directions (we elaborate possible directions in the "Choosing Elements to Monitor" section below).

On the negative side, assessing classroom talk poses numerous ethical, logistical, cultural, and social problems. If the goal is students' talking to learn, or learning through talk, then making participation high-stakes runs the risk of rewarding "display talk" that merely regurgitates what is already known. How is it possible to

# Figure 4.1. Socratic Seminar Holistic Participation Rubric

| | |
|---|---|
| *Participation is outstanding* | • Participant offers enough solid analysis, without prompting, to move the conversation forward<br>• Participant, through his or her comments, demonstrates a deep knowledge of the text and the question<br>• Participant has come to the seminar prepared, with notes and a marked/annotated text<br>• Participant, through his or her comments, shows that he or she is actively listening to other participants<br>• He or she offers clarification or follow-up that extends the conversation<br>• Participant's remarks often refer to specific parts of the text |
| *Participation is very good* | • Participant offers solid analysis without prompting<br>• Through his or her comments, participant demonstrates a good knowledge of the text and the question<br>• Participant has come to the seminar prepared with notes or a marked/annotated text<br>• Participant shows that he or she is actively listening to others.<br>• He or she offers clarification or follow-up |
| *Participation is satisfactory* | • Participant offers some analysis, but needs prompting from the seminar leader or others<br>• Through his or her comments, participant demonstrates a general knowledge of the text and the question<br>• Participant is less prepared, with few notes and no marked/annotated text<br>• Participant is actively listening to others but does not offer clarification or follow-up to others' comments<br>• Participant relies more upon his or her opinion and less on the text to drive his or her comments |
| *Participation is not satisfactory* | • Participant offers little commentary<br>• Participant comes to the seminar ill prepared with little understanding of the text and question<br>• Participant does not listen to others, offers no commentary to further the discussion |

*Note:* Reconfigured rubric based on materials retrieved from studyguide.org.

encourage student talk to be "exploratory" (as Barnes [1976] puts it) on the one hand, then turn around and grade it on the other? Doesn't this practice send a mixed message to students?

In addition, many teachers find it difficult to monitor behavior minute by minute while facilitating learning talk. Is it always possible to reliably keep track of each student's participation? Moreover, as with other curricular areas of English (e.g., writing), some students find classroom participation easier than do others. This variation is an issue not only of individual personality but, depending on the community, also of acceptable gender behaviors, community politeness norms (e.g., whether interruption is considered impolite or a signal of high interest and engagement), or other cultural expectations for who participates or how to participate in talk. Peer relationships or conflicts outside the classroom can also influence who feels free to speak, and teachers might not always be aware of these dynamics (Connolly & Smith, 2002). The public nature of talk makes this more of a problem with talk than with reading or writing. Grading can turn student talk into just another way in which school punishes or rewards young people for conditions outside their control.

With these pros and cons in mind, we introduce some possibilities for tracking and evaluating student learning talk, in case you decide this is a good idea for your particular context. As we have made clear, dialogic teaching involves holding discussions about norms for appropriate behavior early and often. It also involves talking with your students about what counts as skillful participation in doing English. *If you do decide you wish to evaluate such participation on an individual level, we suggest that you delay introducing this complication until students have practice in substantive classroom conversations and recognize its pleasures and rewards.*

*Choosing elements to monitor.* As with any assignment, the elements of interaction you choose to emphasize in an evaluation tool signal your priorities. Those priorities can be *procedural*, meaning student behaviors that promote and maintain civil engagement and widespread participation, such as the active listening requirement on Kimberly Longley's holistic participation rubric (Figure 4.1). Other procedural elements could include coming prepared for learning talk, responding to another's comment respectfully, refraining from personal attacks, keeping one's eyes on whoever is speaking, and refraining from interruption. Those priorities can also be *substantive*, meaning they engage students with content knowledge and skills. Again, Kimberly's rubric suggests that participants use analysis to move the conversation forward, or refer to the text. Depending on specific learning goals, you can include prompts that specify preferred topics, such as analysis of character action or relating character action to theme.

While we have initially framed this issue in terms of teacher choice (since teachers are, in the end, responsible for evaluation), we advocate taking a dialogic stance toward assessment and rubrics. For example, you can work with your students to develop rubrics or other means of assessing student learning talk, making sure to focus on the purpose of the specific interaction. Why not invite students to evaluate themselves with the rubrics? What about discussing with students what the rubrics foreground and background in classroom talk? Such activities allow you to teach students how to participate in classroom talk, to maintain the dialogic spirit of your classroom, to provide students with a voice in their own evaluation, and to think critically about how and why classroom talk functions.

*Choosing means of evaluation.* Self, peer, and teacher evaluation can all be used to track individual progress in classroom interaction. Self-evaluation provides an opportunity for self-monitoring. Two examples of such monitoring include reflective writing about one's growth over time in contributing to discussion (e.g., Adler & Rougle, 2005, p. 134) and filling out the same self-evaluation form after each whole-class discussion to note areas of strength and improvement (Matanzo, 1996; O'Donnell-Allen, 2011). Both peer and self-evaluation can hold students accountable for small-group work. For example, students can report on the extent to which they are contributing to, supporting, and extending peer work in small-group talk (nothing need be said about nonparticipation, made evident by the absence of report).

Teachers can use a range of strategies for monitoring talking to learn. We like the discussion map (e.g., Adler & Rougle, 2005). If you make a map of your classroom and note where students are seated, you can use check marks or symbols to indicate participation (responding to question, introducing new topic, uptake, etc.), or draw arrows to indicate direction of comment. You then have a graphic record of participation patterns in your class. Others prefer the checklist, a list of target behaviors with room for tally marks. A variant of that tool is the scoring checklist (Hess & Posselt, 2002), with varying points for contributions of varying difficulty or sophistication. For example, you might score a point for "making a relevant comment," but two points for "recognizing a contradiction in someone else's opinion." Rather than monitoring participation moment by moment, students or teachers can fill out such a rubric immediately following a discussion.

*Choosing How and Whether to Grade Talking to learn.* You can use these assessment instruments to monitor behaviors without assigning point values to them, and many teachers choose that route. For those who want an opportunity for students to earn points, rather than lose them, or who wish to use grades to motivate participation, the decision of how many points to award, and for what, is similar to decisions made for writing assignments or other activities. A holistic rubric provides one model, as does a checklist with both positive points for steps in the desired direction and negative points for such acts as disrespectful speech or monopolizing the conversation.

As you decide how to sequence dialogic learning talk over the course of your semester or year, assessment issues may enter into your deliberation: How, if at all, will I move from nongraded or low-stakes assessment to higher expectations? How, if at all, will I incorporate discussions of assessment and evaluation into meta-lessons? How, if at all, will I grade aspects of preparation for talk or the resulting products?

## PLANNING FOR DIALOGIC INSTRUCTION AT THE LEVEL OF THE UNIT

If a semester or year course involves the coherent development of a set of concepts and skills, then a unit provides a means for developing a major course idea and smaller set of skills and knowledge (see text box).

### A Closer Look: Resources for Achieving Coherence in Unit Planning

Several authors inspire our thinking about coherence in designing units and courses:

- *Curriculum as Conversation: Transforming Traditions of Teaching and Learning,* by Arthur Applebee (University of Chicago Press, 1996). Applebee combines the idea of coherence with the idea that teaching English language arts involves engaging in conversation with the living traditions of reading and discussing significant texts. In his metaphor, conversations take place on both a daily basis and among texts and concepts across the curriculum.
- *Teaching English by Design: How to Create and Carry out Instructional Units,* by Peter Smagorinsky (Heinemann, 2008). Smagorinsky promotes the use of "conceptual units," periods of time dedicated to "sustained attention to a related set of ideas" (p. 111). Conceptual units are marked by backward planning from your ultimate instructional goals, dialogic activities, and major assessments that teach as well as provide data for assessment.
- *Engaging Readers and Writers with Inquiry: Promoting Deep Understandings in Language Arts and the Content Areas with Guiding Questions,* by Jeffrey Wilhelm (Scholastic, 2007). Wilhelm uses the term *inquiry units* instead of *conceptual units,* but the focus is very similar: Units cohere around an essential question, and activities within the units promote dialogue around each question. The questions are primarily the teacher's questions, posed around central issues in the discipline.
- *What's the Big Idea? Question-Driven Units to Motivate Reading, Writing, and Thinking,* by Jim Burke (Heinemann, 2010). Burke also organizes the curriculum around questions related to the big ideas in a subject but focuses on developing the ability of students to question, to make them more critical and independent thinkers.

All books highlighted in the text box advocate planning around a big idea or a major objective. Sometimes your department or district defines objectives and topics for you, but your task is still to find the particular way in, guided by your knowledge of your own students. Imagine you teach 9th-grade English and you are required to teach *Romeo and Juliet* 2nd semester. Objectives may well accompany this requirement, such as providing an introduction to Shakespeare's life and times, introducing students to the idea of tragedy, and exploring Shakespeare's characters. How can you take a dialogic stance in turning this rather academic and disparate set of objectives into a coherent unit that will engage 9th-graders?

Such a rich literary text opens many possibilities for dialogue:

- Conflicts driving plot and character development (romantic love vs. family obligations, civil obedience vs. honor, secrecy vs. transparency)
- Values and gender roles held in the 16th century and the present (use current versions of this story in dialogue with the original play)
- Historical controversies surrounding Shakespeare's identity.

Many options for final projects for a *Romeo and Juliet* unit are widely available in print and online resources for teachers. Having all these great resources, however, can make the task of focusing your unit even more daunting.

You might decide on a performance-based project putting the 16th and 21st centuries into dialogue. Your final project may entail small acting groups each developing and performing a short scene placing Shakespeare's dialogue in a modern-day situation. Perhaps students will keep a writing and rehearsal journal as they read the play, choose their scene, and develop it for performance. Each student might also write a short essay explaining his or her character's perspectives and actions in relation to the play's meaning and the group's interpretation.

Figure 4.2 presents an annotated outline of a unit that both builds toward the final performances and builds in opportunities for students to engage in dialogic interaction over the course of studying the play, using dialogic tools that offer opportunities for students to prepare for, practice, and reflect on talking to learn. Note that you can adapt this unit in various ways, depending on the needs and interests of your particular students.

Our *Romeo and Juliet* unit example is intended to illustrate how a dialogic stance can operate at the level of the unit in ways that will support your efforts at generating more dialogic participation at the classroom interaction level. As your academic objectives and your goals for dialogic interaction work together over the year, so your units help you build toward those goals in smaller steps. Activities within the unit become experiences you have created for student learning.

# Figure 4.2. Sample Unit Outline for *Romeo and Juliet*

*Romeo and Juliet* Unit

*Essential Question:* Have love and social conflict changed since Shakespeare's time?
*Learning Objectives:* Students will be able to

- Read and discuss Shakespeare's *Romeo and Juliet*, showing both literal understanding and personal interpretation of characters and their actions.
- Analyze a short scene and prepare it for performance, explaining how the analysis led to particular choices in acting, directing, and design.
- Engage in whole-class discussion of themes and action.
- Make productive use of small-group time in preparing a scene for performance.
- Prepare for discussion through careful reading, note-taking, and writing questions on selected readings.
- Write an essay that demonstrates understanding of Shakespeare's language through its interpretation in one scene.

*Bullets 3, 4, and 5 define objectives for growth in dialogic interaction.*

*Final Project: 50% credit for group-work; 50% credit for individual work*

In groups of three or four, students will

1. Choose a short scene (40–60 lines) from *Romeo and Juliet*.
2. Choose a modern-day setting for the scene and write up an explanation of the context.
3. Block and rehearse the scene in the original language.
4. Using props, costume pieces, and simple furniture, perform the scene for the class.

Individual work

1. Write a self-evaluation of the work done by self and group.
2. Write responses to two other scenes performed by classmates.
3. Write an essay explaining one character's perspective on the scene and what he or she was trying to achieve.

*The unit activities build toward the final project, and activities and final project together are designed to achieve the unit objectives.*

*(continued)*

71

Figure 4.2. (continued)

*Negotiating meaning and performance choices is a dialogic activity taking place within each small group.*

*This final Socratic seminar provides an opportunity for students to create classroom knowledge by drawing on the work they have done over several weeks.*

*The anticipation guide is a teacher-led tool. Although students have engaged in student-led activity in previous units, teacher-structured and led activity is quite appropriate at the beginning of the unit, before students have had a chance to become familiar with the play.*

*Dialogues between yesterday and today, between Romeo and Juliet and versions of the story, and among the various 20th-century means of presenting the story are recorded in each student's notes and become the basis for whole-group discussion. Students can refer to them to make points, or to compose student-written questions.*

Unit activities

- Pre-reading anticipation guide: Given eight values statements related to issues in the play, each student will mark a position between "strongly agree" and "strongly disagree" and be ready to explain the choice in a Four Corners activity.
- While reading play: Students will keep a chart recording reactions to the filmed scenes shown in class. At least once during each act, the teacher will show two contrasting scenes from filmed versions of *Romeo and Juliet* (Luhrman, 1996) or a modernized version of the story (e.g., *West Side Story, Romeo Must Die, Simba's Pride*). These notes will form the basis for whole-class discussions occurring each week of the unit.
- In small groups, students will choose and prepare their scene for performance, following norms for respectful and productive small-group interaction established earlier in the year.
- During performances, students will be taking notes and completing peer evaluations of each other's scenes.
- After reading and performances: students will participate in a culminating Socratic seminar on the essential question, "Have love and social conflict changed since Shakespeare's time?"

*Reading and writing peer "reviews" of performance is another form of dialogue, by this point by an audience that is well acquainted with the play and its performance history.*

72

# Aligning Learning Talk and Assignments with a Dialogic Stance

You are in the kitchen once again. At this point, you've assembled a variety of tools and have a vision for your long-term diet and eating habits. The question now arises, What do you want to make? English teachers aren't like boutique chefs who specialize in just one food. English teachers must prepare for students a varied diet of learning experiences: In addition to the traditional fare of grammar, vocabulary, literature study, and writing, we are increasingly expected to help students develop literacy skills in other areas as well. A good portion of the professional development literature on student learning talk and discussion focuses on literature study. Literature study may be the hamburger of your classroom—that is, a staple frequently on the menu—and you'll find plenty of examples of student talk in literature study throughout this book. But we also want to emphasize that a dialogic stance on teaching can be infused into every "dish" you serve.

Increasingly, English as a subject area encompasses teaching a wide range of written texts; teaching students to read and interpret a broad range of genres beyond fictional literature; exploring rapid shifts in how technologies mediate both reading and writing today; and understanding how diverse and shifting world Englishes (with different grammars and so on) shape the ever-changing global landscape of reading, writing, speaking, and listening. A consensus is growing that working with a broad array of text types and practices—beyond the fictional literary study and analysis showcased in many examples throughout the book—prepares secondary students for academic work in college and for civic, family, work, and other lifelong literacy engagements beyond school. A particular focus in diversifying English curriculum, and a top priority in the Common Core State Standards (CCSS) on writing, is the teaching—not merely assigning—of argument writing (e.g., CCSS Initiative, 2010). We take argument writing as our focus here, although some facets of our discussion may also apply to teaching other types of writing.

Other books provide guidance for the nuts and bolts of setting up talk about writing in various formats (such as small-group peer review talk, one-on-one teacher conferences, collaborative writing talk, and whole-class discussions or debates) within a dialogic framework (e.g., Adler & Rougle, 2005). This chapter, by contrast, fundamentally rethinks writing instruction from a dialogic perspective.

It reinforces the idea of going beyond the interpersonal level to consider dialogic instruction at the curricular level, an idea introduced in Chapter 4. We show how to take a dialogic stance toward writing itself in crafting courses, units, and assignments. The example of Libby Ancheta shows how the best intentions to go dialogic can fall short when a teacher finds herself constrained by a form-focused writing assignment. Lucia Elden illustrates how to see argument writing more broadly as a dialogic activity—when crafting a course syllabus or unit plan, when designing an assignment, and when devising and adapting dialogic tools to support argument writing development.

## THE FORMALIST APPROACH:
## TALKING TO MASTER THE FIVE-PARAGRAPH THEME

Many secondary English teachers take a formalist approach to teaching writing, including argument writing. By *formalist*, we mean instruction emphasizing the form an argument takes rather than its thematic and logical content. Critics of formalist instruction have long argued that emphasizing argumentative form fails to invite students to practice reasoning about issues, for example, by examining underlying beliefs in support of evidence given in support or opposition to given claims (e.g., Hillocks, 2011). Critics further charge that formalist approaches fail to invite students to qualify arguments or take moderate, nuanced, or even collegial stances on important social issues; rather, formalist approaches to teaching and writing argument can push students toward extreme, polarizing stances—a societal trend we discussed in Chapter 1 that dialogic teaching can work against. While these criticisms may be worth putting aside when teaching students to tackle timed essay-writing tasks (e.g., standardized tests), formalist instruction rarely prepares students for writing high-impact, real-world arguments, including arguments professors ask them to write in college courses.

No assignment structure better exemplifies and drives formalist approaches to argument than that omnipresent classroom fixture, the five-paragraph theme. Johnson, Thompson, Smagorinsky, and Fry (2003) suggest that the five-paragraph theme endures in secondary classrooms for several reasons. First, it has historical momentum in schools. If university and college writing instructors and teacher educators fail to teach preservice teachers other powerful approaches to argument writing or its instruction, new teachers will default to what prevails in the school cultures they enter. When they begin learning to teach in schools, new teachers quickly learn from mentors that teaching the five-paragraph theme is the easiest way to get students to produce well-organized, easy-to-read texts. Moreover, mounting institutional pressures on teachers (e.g., for high test scores, for greater efficiency, for alignment with building- or districtwide requirements) further recommend the five-paragraph theme as the easiest route to helping many students write readable arguments (p. 138).

Libby Ancheta was a new teacher who used a five-paragraph theme assignment when she taught argument writing for the first time—her first draft of argument-writing instruction. With the pressures of standards for teaching written argument upon her (for many U.S. teachers, those forces now include the CCSS [2010] for argument), Libby worked closely with a mentor teacher who had been teaching at the school for decades and was nearing retirement. She gave Libby previous five-paragraph themes she had used, declaring, "These kids really need structure!" Libby also consulted the schoolwide guidelines for argument writing. The "Take a Stand" five-paragraph theme assignment she developed is available at vbrr.wiki.educ.msu.edu/.

As Libby frames it, the goal of the writing is to take and develop support for a position on the issue of capital punishment. The assignment suggests five steps for generating essay material:

- Read a pro/con article;
- Decide on one of two positions;
- Pick support for the position from the article;
- Pick a counterargument to refute; and
- Write it all up.

To support student learning talk through the assignment, Libby wanted to go dialogic. She decided to help students generate ideas about the pros and cons of capital punishment through what she called a Socratic seminar. She first had them read a short pair of pro/con articles about capital punishment from the *New York Times*. She then divided the class into two sections, one side for, one against, capital punishment. The two groups faced one another in the dialogue. The Socratic seminar gave them an opportunity to hear others' perspectives on the topic. It also helped them reason about their own perspectives.

TARA: All right. It says, at least 124 people have been freed from death row after evidence of their innocence emerged, so like they were going to like kill them or whatever but then they found out they were innocent.
AMANDA: Well they didn't die in there.
. . .
TED: So what if their time was shorter . . .
TERRENCE: Yeah like that's what I am saying . . . like you guys just want to sentence them and kill them.
TED: Exactly so . . .
AMANDA: No we are saying if there is enough evidence . . . that's what we said yesterday . . . if there is enough evidence.
TED: Well I don't understand what enough evidence is . . .
TARA: Well there was enough evidence to put them on death row and then they figured out . . .

TALULAH: On death row . . .

TARA: I don't know, I am just saying.

TED: Yeah like it was saying it actually takes a long time for them to actually get killed, so like when we say if they are like murderers then we should like keep them 20 years and it's all just going to add up before and all this crap . . . it is still going to be a long time.

CALVIN: Yeah, but even when they are waiting to be trialed for whatever they did, killing them, it's just going to be a lot faster than 12 years and keeping them for a life sentence so if they are there for 12 years or 30 years, 12 years is a lot less than 30 years.

Students are talking to learn in this example, but what are they learning? First, they practice aligning themselves with available pro/con positions, a skill that will serve them in writing a formulaic argument, such as a five-paragraph theme. Second, they are articulating reasons for that position or for why the opposing position is wrong (i.e., "At least 124 people have been freed from death row after evidence of their innocence emerged"), also needed for the five-paragraph theme genre. Third, they are learning to argue strongly polarized positions (either *for* or *against* capital punishment), another requirement of the five-paragraph theme assignment. Students learn these skills as they listen to and respond to the words and ideas of others, both classmates and the authors of the articles and models they have read in preparation for the Socratic seminar.

This sort of talk undoubtedly prepares students to do well on the writing sections of standardized tests, and for many students, that is not a trivial goal. Such talk does not, however, prepare them for the kinds of writing needed for college, careers, and most domains of life beyond school. While Libby's Socratic seminar does a good job of supporting the task of the assignment, her capacity to go dialogic is limited, because *the five-paragraph theme assignment inherited from her mentor doesn't frame argument writing as dialogic in nature.* Formalist assignments ignore the fundamentally social purposes of written argument. In the "real world" of family, career, citizen, and other walks of life and in the practice of academic writing for college, however, written arguments offer responses to the words, ideas, and arguments of others and they anticipate responses from others.

Writing, on this view, becomes a tool for entering into dialogue with others or "What I say (in writing) responds to what you said (in writing)," to modify our mantra from Chapter 1. When teachers frame writing tasks as fundamentally dialogic, then it makes more sense for learning talk to involve qualifying arguments and taking moderate, nuanced, and collegial stances. When teachers break the mold of formalist assignments like the five-paragraph theme, learning talk can also focus more on reasoning about the underlying beliefs that would hold up or disconfirm evidence given in support or opposition to capital punishment (e.g., the sanctity of life principle).

## Logical Reasoning: Talking to Learn Informal Reasoning Skills

The logical reasoning approach to teaching argument invites students to dialogue with peers and teacher to learn the informal reasoning skills needed to write persuasive arguments (Hillocks, 2011). According to philosopher of language Stephen Toulmin (1958), those skills include marshaling evidence (also called data) to support claims (or conclusions); explaining why given evidence supports a claim (what Toulmin called warrants); supporting the warrant, or backing; articulating the limitations and boundaries of the arguments, or "qualifiers"; and anticipating objections and counterarguments to craft rebuttals. The conceptual underpinning for Toulmin's informal logical approach derives from Aristotle (1991). The approach focuses on the internal reasoning of an argumentative text, but also on the context-dependent aspects of argumentation and persuasion. To persuade someone to believe that a given piece or set of evidence supports a claim, the model suggests, you must appeal to a more foundational set of beliefs they hold about how the world works—called the grounding for an argument. Often, those foundational sets of beliefs depend on the context: What a group in one setting unthinkingly takes for granted as a true statement about how the world works, another group across the globe completely refuses to accept.

The context-dependent aspects of argumentative grounding also depend upon rhetorical purposes. Consider, for example, three key types of purposes for which one might need to craft arguments:

- Forensic. Situations involving judgment about past actions. For example, courtroom arguments, murder mysteries, and (to use a classroom example) plagiarism cases.
- Deliberative. Situations involving decisions about future policies or courses of action. For example, legislative arguments or deliberations about new policies for schools.
- Ceremonial. Situations involving affirmation of a person or community. For example, an obituary written to honor someone who has died or a brief speech given during a ribbon-cutting ceremony.

Each of those situations—or rhetorical purposes for argument—in turn, calls for different argumentation strategies and potentially different kinds of learning talk. For example, situations requiring deliberation involve people in imagining and speculating about the future, articulating shared values, weighing various options and trade-offs, and compromising. As we noted already, many lawmakers seem not to engage in such learning talk around important deliberations involving our lives together.

Consult Hillocks (2011) to learn more about structuring learning talk about argument writing that will help students learn informal reasoning skills.

We know of two alternatives to the formalist approach that push students into deeper learning talk about argumentation. The Logical Reasoning approach described in the text box has been much discussed in the professional literature (e.g., Hillocks, 2011). However, that approach and the accompanying terminology of informal logic can seem difficult or too arcane for new teachers to master. Like the formalist approach, it backgrounds the fundamentally social nature of argument writing: "What I say responds to what you said." Thus, the next section focuses on a third approach to teaching argument writing: conversational entry.

## CONVERSATIONAL ENTRY: SOCIAL MOVES FOR CONTRIBUTING TO ACADEMIC AND OTHER CONVERSATIONS

The conversational entry approach brings the dialogic stance more fully into writing instruction by foregrounding the inherently social nature of writing. Before getting into learning talk about writing, let's consider what the dialogic stance means for understanding the act and nature of writing itself. The rhetorician and literary critic Kenneth Burke (1972) famously described the process of entering into a parlor conversation:

> Imagine that you enter a parlor. You come late. When you arrive, others have long preceded you, and they are engaged in a heated discussion, a discussion too heated for them to pause and tell you exactly what it is about. In fact, the discussion had already begun long before any of them got there, so that no one present is qualified to retrace for you all the steps that had gone before. You listen for a while, until you decide that you have caught the tenor of the argument; then you put in your oar. Someone answers; you answer him; another comes to your defense; another aligns himself against you, to either the embarrassment or gratification of your opponent, depending upon the quality of your ally's assistance. However, the discussion is interminable. The hour grows late, you must depart. And you do depart, with the discussion still vigorously in progress. (pp. 110–111)

This conversational parlor metaphor reframes argument writing as taking a turn in an unending conversation. Entering into and departing from that ongoing conversation requires skillful social maneuvering.

From this view, writing an argument requires writers to figure out the social maneuvering needed to enter into a written dialogue with others. As Burke's metaphor suggests, that social maneuvering can be practiced through learning talk. In college writing, as we will see below, such conversation is often academic in nature. The parlor then represents a community of scholars or students discussing a set of issues among themselves. The task of teaching argument, from this view, involves equipping students with some basic skills for entering into specific academic conversations—what are increasingly being called *disciplinary literacies*

(Langer, 2010). Students practice skills needed for entering into disciplinary conversations through face-to-face learning talk, which scaffolds them into the moves they need to make as writers. Teachers introduce brief templates to help students practice those moves. For example: "On the one hand, _____ argues _____. On the other hand, _____ contends _____. Others even maintain _____. My own view is _____" (Graff & Birkenstein, 2009, p. 222). Introducing templates such as these can help students learn to approach academic arguments as composed of "dialogic moves" that respond to the moves and stances of others.

## An Example of Conversational Entry: Lucia's Community College Classroom

Let's now look more closely at how such a dialogic stance plays out in the work of a veteran writing teacher, Lucia Elden. For several years, Lucia has been teaching a writing course at a community college that enrolls high school students from a nearby high school. The dual-enrollment program aims to improve college readiness and bolster college enrollment rates for the secondary students. In her syllabus, Lucia explicitly framed one of the two central course goals in dialogic terms:

> You will learn to write by adjusting your rhetorical style depending on who you are writing to, especially learning to write for an academic discourse community in which you will make idea and source connections and write for those who might not know you.

In other words, she aimed to make the social rules of academic writing more explicit and visible for her students, most of whom had not been well prepared to succeed in college-level writing. To make these rules for argument writing more explicit, Lucia did not emphasize the five-paragraph theme. Instead, she invited students to explore different rhetorical styles and to actively participate in and contribute to an "academic discourse community."

Lucia structured the exploration of rhetorical styles and active contribution to an academic discourse community through a sequence of review and response writing. Students began by choosing an academic article about an issue that interested them. They wrote two argumentative reviews for the class and uploaded them on the course management platform. The first review was an "informal" review of the article written for friends and the second was a formal academic review written for professors. We'll focus here on the first task.

In preparation for the informal review, students studied the genre by looking online and posting reviews about movies, video games, and restaurants and by agreeing or disagreeing with the posted reviews of others. Lucia and her students also studied reviews in magazines together—analyzing various rhetorical stylistic features. After posting the "informal" reviews, each student replied to another student's review in the Discussion Forum, using more formal academic discourse. The prompt for that assignment read:

Click on a new discussion topic and post the title of your review. Upload the review. Respond to at least one colleague's review. . . . Reply to a classmate (using Graff and Birkenstein's templates) by using your author. For example:

> While Tannen believes that classroom participation can be seen as different due to gender and culture, bell hooks or Jamaica Kincaid would say that classroom participation is also determined by class. In some ways socioeconomic status is more important in determining familiarity with academic culture and codes of behavior and would affect a student's classroom participation.

What kind of talk or interaction did students need to engage in to accomplish the kind of argument writing Lucia invited? Table 5.1 presents a dialogic tool (based on the templates of Graff and Birkenstein, 2009, pp. 221–235) for helping students practice entering into academic conversations. The chart breaks down various dialogic moves that successful academic speakers and writers make. It was these moves Lucia wanted her students to practice orally before diving into their writing response task.

Working with transitions is a key idea of the conversational entry approach to structuring learning talk. Practicing transitions in classroom dialogues encouraged students to articulate relationships among various positions and speakers. For example, Lucia modeled and students then practiced simple dialogic moves in classroom discussion. They used the templates in the text box, having fun with fancy words like *deplore* and other formal language that seems more natural written than spoken. They also departed from the templates, however, for example, through such simple positioning moves as, "Like Kyle, I . . . " Through a combination of template-guided and improvised talk, Lucia invited students to practice seeing themselves in new ways as writers.

She also used problems they brought up, about their lives as first-year college students, to practice the transitioning and social maneuvering moves. They brainstormed around generative themes (Freire, 1970), elicited through open-ended questions about students' lives in college. Consider the following reconstructed transcript, made from Lucia's memory (unlike all the other transcripts in the book made from video or audio recordings):

TEACHER: So what are some problems that you or friends of yours have encountered as college freshmen?
DANIELLE: Shyness can be a problem.
TEACHER: So how can we understand shyness? How can a teacher understand it?
DANIELLE: Well, I was really shy in my first semester, but I am not shy anymore. I feel like it is my money and so I am going to speak up or ask a question.

## Table 5.1. Dialogic Moves for Entering into Academic Conversations

| Dialogic Moves | Templates (Examples) |
|---|---|
| *Moves for Establishing Significance* | |
| Indicating who cares | "If sports enthusiasts stopped to think about it, many of them might simply assume that the most successful athletes _____. However, new research shows _____." (p. 231) |
| Establishing why your claims matter | "Although X may seem of concern to only a small group of _____, it should in fact concern anyone who cares about _____." (p. 231) |
| *Moves for Introducing Others' Views* | |
| Introducing what others say | "It has become common today to dismiss _____." (p. 221) |
| Introducing standard views | "Conventional wisdom has it that _____." (p. 221) |
| Introducing something implied or assumed | "Although X does not say so directly, she apparently assumes that _____." (p. 222) |
| *Moves for Paraphrasing and Quoting Others* | |
| Capturing authorial action | "X deplores the tendency to _____." (p. 223) |
| Introducing quotations | "As the prominent philosopher X puts it, " '_____.' " (p. 224) |
| Explaining quotations | "X's point is that _____." (p. 225) |
| *Moves for Positioning Oneself in Relation to Others' Ideas* | |
| Disagreeing, with reasons | "I disagree with X's view that _____ because, as recent research has shown, _____." (p. 225) |
| Agreeing, with a difference | "If group X is right that _____, as I think they are, then we need to reassess the popular assumptions that _____." (p. 226) |
| Agreeing and disagreeing simultaneously | "I'm of two minds about X's claim that _____. On the one hand, I agree that _____. On the other hand, I'm not sure if _____." (p. 227) |
| Signaling who is saying what | "My own view, however, is that _____." (p. 227) |
| *Moves for Anticipating and Responding to Potential Objections* | |
| Entertaining objections | "Of course, many will probably disagree with this assertion that _____." (p. 228) |
| Naming your naysayers | "Although not all *Christians* think alike, some of them will probably dispute my claim that _____." (p. 229) |
| Making concessions while still standing your ground | "Proponents of X are right to argue that _____. But they exaggerate when they claim that _____." (p. 230) |

*Source*: Graff & Birkenstein (2009)

TEACHER: So Wendy, are you saying that students can get more comfortable the more they are in college?

DANIELLE: Yes, that's right. But I'm not sure about comfortable, just okay.

TEACHER: Does anyone have a different or similar perspective?

MARK: [Legs constantly moving.] I think it is totally about the instructor. Some classes I feel totally shut down and I never speak. But in this one, of course, I'm always talking.

TEACHER: Is it the format? Is it that we are used to each other?

MARK: Well, you ask questions and want answers and I like to talk.

TEACHER: What if a person doesn't want to talk? Does that limit their learning in any way? Andy, what do you think?

ANDY: I don't think so. Some people like to listen.

KANDY: But a shy person is going to have problems no matter what.

JONATHAN: I don't think we can call anyone a shy person, just like when we were talking the other day about illegal immigrants. A person isn't shy all the time, like they aren't illegal first as a person.

TEACHER: That is really an interesting insight, Jonathan. It sounds like what some of you are talking about is classroom circumstances that cause students not to participate?

CASSADAY: I read about how the Japanese culture communicates all in one stretch, whoever has the floor and no one interrupts them, so if others were talking some students would not want to interrupt. Plus, in that Deborah Tannen article we read, she said that boys like to argue and debate and will talk a lot.

RACHEL: I disagree with that. In my classes, girls talk just as much.

TEACHER: What do the rest of you think? We will talk about this some more on Thursday. But can you all see that we have created a synthesis discussion, just like we are working on in our papers?

Students themselves introduced a topic for problem-posing talk, although Lucia strongly guided the subsequent direction, encouraging students to respond to one another's ideas and to ideas of authors they had read. Together the students considered various perspectives on the problem under discussion, using transitions (such as Rachel's "I disagree with that") to connect new argumentative stances with previous claims—in this case, a claim made by Deborah Tannen. Lucia asked provocative questions (e.g., "What if a person doesn't want to talk? Does that limit their learning in any way? Andy, what do you think?") and enthusiastically noticed the process of their talk: "Can you all see that we have created a synthesis discussion, just like we are working on in our papers?" She also made explicit that they were practicing in their talk some of the moves she wanted to see them make in written arguments.

Another way of practicing the social maneuvering of different argumentative stances is a "talk show" task. Students think about the connections between various speakers and actually moderate, write, and perform the responses. Such practice transitioning talk and text, in tandem with a dialogically oriented writing task like Lucia's, encourages students to respond to ideas in the text *and also* to one another as interpreters who use texts written by others for their own conversational purposes. Lucia used an online discussion board in the course management system to structure the technology of the writing task. This technology meant that students were "talking" to one another in writing—directly to individual writers, but also more broadly to all other class members who were potential audience members of each discussion board post. As students advanced interpretations of nonfiction texts to dialogue with one another (with the template tool in hand), they responded to one another's ideas and words indirectly (Bakhtin, 1981).

In this process, students can take stances in relation to the texts and to one another as knowledgeable, active contributors to an academic conversation. Consider, for example, the following piece of writing that emerged in response to Lucia's assignment:

> Danielle,
>
> Your article and mine are somewhat similar, as they both have to do with male and female gender stereotypes. You mention that the author of your article relates the language of feminism and the word *power*, yet I did not get a feeling of feminism from your informal review. . . . [I] found the sentence, "Normally in a relationship men tend to feel a sense of domination over their woman while having sex," extremely stereotypical. The author of my article, Emily Martin, would have had a heart attack if she had read that sentence. Martin, I believe, would have quickly pointed out that a woman is certainly not a man's possession, and that it is wrong to stereotype a male/female sexual relationship (especially when a man dominates a woman), since every sexual relationship is different.
>
> I did enjoy however, the fact that you pointed out that the word *power* can be associated with other words (both negative and positive) that can change the way power makes you feel. You are right in believing that a language of power exists and that it should be taken more seriously.
>
> Rachael

Rachael enters into an academic conversation using a number of dialogic moves requiring considerable sensitivity to the social situation of writing. She highlights the social nature of the exchange by formatting her response as a letter written to Danielle. She begins by articulating a common theme or concern (male and female gender stereotypes) that Danielle's writing shares with her own—and one that the class had touched upon in the discussion above. She frames her argument as a response to a claim made by Danielle (that "the author of your article relates the language of feminism and the word 'power'"), introduces her authorial stance on the topic ("yet I did not get a feeling of feminism from your informal review"), and goes on to rather cleverly mobilize an author she had read to voice her critique ("The author of my article, Emily Martin, would have had a heart attack if she had read that sentence"). She concludes by noting a point of agreement. These moves produce a moderate and somewhat nuanced, rather than polarizing, argumentative stance. Equipped with templates and transitions, she seeks out points where she can articulate commonality with the writer and she develops a short argument around her disagreement with the author's stance. She thus succeeds in making a collegial, yet quite critical, argument in response to Danielle.

## A Few Further Considerations

Template tools, such as those Lucia shared with students, are indicative rather than comprehensive—meaning that students or teachers should not be locked into using only this language (which can become formulaic to the point of meaninglessness). Teachers and students alike can discover new moves and they can create their own templates, as Lucia's students did. What matters is the explicit mentoring of students into working with those moves in low-stakes talk and writing. Such practice, over time, can cultivate a "What I say (in writing) responds to what you said (in writing)" stance.

If students think about writing as inherently dialogic, they can still be hosts (vs. active contributors) to a dialogue in their writing. As host of a dialogue, an argument writer might summarize and revoice the words and ideas of others—as can sometimes happen in the talk show task. Libby's assignment invited such a "host" stance. Even though she directed students to "take a stand" (either for or against capital punishment), the assignment and the talk about the issue failed to invest them with inventive powers to contribute something *new* to the ongoing dialogue about the issue. To make that goal easier to reach, try inviting argumentative writing focused in on local issues and situations where students' voices might actually make a difference, such as

- A school without a recycling program;
- Community or school programs (e.g., athletic, drama, music) on the chopping block;
- Polluted local streams or parks;
- A school or community library in need of more books; or
- School or community policies surrounding school shootings (see also Duke et al., 2012, pp. 143–144).

Sometimes teachers balk at the conversational entry approach laid out here, because it can seem formulaic and uncreative, much like the five-paragraph theme. However, the approach—at its best—empowers students with a social vision for writing and offers them an accompanying set of dialogic tools for achieving social work through written argument. Indeed, we have used the templates as dialogic tools in our work with graduate students who need to master new argumentative writing moves to enter into new academic discourses and, in the process, launch professional academic careers. Finally, the conversational entry approach can perhaps most support students, such as multilinguals who write and speak languages beyond Dominant American English (DAE) and may find the conventions of academic argument writing in DAE strange and distancing.

## A Closer Look: Coauthorship

When some people think of a dialogic approach to writing, they may think of students writing together. Developing collaborative argument writing skills can help students practice the kinds of writing they can expect to do in college, careers, and beyond, qualifying it as a critical "21st literacy skill." In your workplace, for example, you might find yourself collaboratively writing:

- A research paper assignment that two sections of 10th-grade English will both complete;
- A proposal to a local foundation for funding for classroom technology, written with the school media specialist;
- A revised English curriculum oriented around the Common Core State Standards;
- A memo to the principal, from the English department, about writing across the curriculum; and
- Emails to parents from a teaching team.

While we do not focus in depth on this approach to argument writing, we—as coauthors of this book and several other articles about our shared interests and work—have ourselves found that the whole of an argument is usually greater than the sum of its individual contributions. Admittedly, it often takes more work to make the multiple voices and perspectives of a coauthored piece hang together. We think it's worth it.

Technologies like Google Drive, Dropbox, and Wikispaces can be terrific resources for collaborative composition of arguments:

- Google Drive (drive.google.com): allows authors to work simultaneously on a document, but formatting can be a challenge. We love the commenting function as an affordance for opening dialogue among members of a writing team and between teachers and student writers. FREE.
- Dropbox (www.dropbox.com): allows authors to format documents in Word and build a document collaboratively but does not allow authors to work simultaneously on a document like Google Drive. FREE.
- Wikispaces (www.wikispaces.com): allows authors to collaboratively write and share materials, such as evidence and sources for an argument they are developing. Provides a place to exchange video documents. FREE.

# *Transforming Practice Through Dialogic Inquiry*

Up to this point, you've encountered examples of dialogic teaching in a variety of contexts and found tools for initiating and maintaining student involvement in learning talk across the English language arts curriculum. In Part III, you'll find ways to move your dialogic teaching to the next level by nurturing your own professional development. Chapter 6 provides easy-to-follow directions on how to conduct dialogic discourse analyses of talk in your classroom, with examples from teachers' self-study. We hope you'll find discourse analysis as valuable as the teachers we worked with have found it: Looking closely at the language you and your students are actually using can push you toward higher-quality teaching and learning talk.

Chapter 7 reflects our experience that learning to teach dialogically can be a dialogic process itself. Make changes in your teaching practices stick through self-initiated, collaborative professional development that you sustain and embed in your everyday classroom practice. You'll find details about how to set up professional learning communities (PLCs) to share your struggles and successes and to grow together as dialogic teachers.

CHAPTER 6

# Transforming Practice Through Discourse Analysis

After a big game you can often find professional athletes in the team video room reviewing footage with coaches and other players. They watch a clip, rewind it, and watch it again in slow motion to analyze, evaluate, and discuss. Video makes it possible to freeze a moment in time for more careful consideration. Video analysis has become common in competitive sports because it offers a powerful tool for helping athletes study and improve their performance. Similarly, careful analysis of the play-by-play action of the classroom can be just as effective for helping you improve your own practice.

When NBA players watch film, they might analyze players' techniques, examine how well the team carried out particular plays, or evaluate how well their defense measured up to the opposing team's offense. While athletes examine plays and technique, dialogic teachers who wish to improve their practice focus in particular on classroom talk. You might, for example, analyze the number of students who participated, the number of uptake or authentic questions asked, or the quality of students' responses. Just as video provides athletes with a freeze frame of action from the game, transcripts of classroom discussion make it possible to closely examine the dynamics of classroom interactions.

Specifically, this chapter focuses on discourse analysis, the study of language-in-use. Like others in the field, we see discourse analysis as a powerful tool for helping teachers improve their practice (e.g., Rex & Schiller, 2009; Rymes, 2009). This chapter introduces a way of examining classroom talk with an eye toward achieving dialogic learning talk: *dialogic classroom discourse analysis*. We identify specific indicators to look for in your classroom talk to determine the extent to which you are achieving dialogic learning talk in your classroom.

To illustrate the process of dialogic classroom discourse analysis, we share experiences of two classroom teachers, Madelyn Napier and Krista Delafuente, as they

- Identify an area of focus;
- Videorecord a classroom interaction;
- Select and transcribe a short clip;
- Analyze the transcript; and
- Revise their practice.

89

As you read about their experiences, we invite you to explore the process for yourself. How you apply dialogic classroom discourse analysis, however, will of course depend on your own curricular and instructional goals. Therefore, we suggest many ways to explore classroom talk in your own classroom.

## IDENTIFY AN AREA OF FOCUS

The process of dialogic classroom discourse analysis is most fruitful when we focus on something that challenges us. Rather than looking at your best work, we recommend zeroing in on something that is bugging you. Even if you do not fully understand or cannot yet fully articulate what the challenge is, you can start this process by following your intuition. For example:

- Have you noticed that discussions in your 5th-period class fall flat?
- Do you feel that you could be getting more out of discussions about literature?
- Does a particular group of students challenge you more than others?
- Are you dissatisfied with the level of participation from students?

These are the kinds of puzzles that will likely lead you down a productive path. It might be helpful to keep a journal over the course of a week or a couple of weeks to help you process your ideas and identify a focus.

## VIDEORECORD A CLASSROOM INTERACTION

The next step is to videorecord a lesson related to your area of focus—and then to watch that video. A few issues to consider:

- *Equipment:* You can achieve quality results with digital video cameras, flip cameras, or laptop cameras. Use whatever equipment is most comfortable and convenient for you.
- *Disclosure*: While some teachers prefer to tell their students what they are up to, other teachers who strive for "unedited" student behavior opt to place the camera inconspicuously and keep their recording private. See the text box below for further discussion of the ethical issues surrounding such choices.
- *Camera angle:* While some teachers prefer to direct the camera at themselves and focus on their own moves and technique, others prefer to position the camera at the back of the room to capture an unfamiliar vantage point.
- *Audio:* Make sure your audio records loud and clear by testing the audio before recording your classroom talk.

## A Closer Look: Privacy and Confidentiality

Videotaping students and making that video available to others can be a minefield in terms of protecting students' privacy and confidentiality rights. Here are some tips.

- Know the policies of your school or district regarding videotaping. Some districts have opt-out charters. In these districts, videotaping students at any time is an accepted practice unless the parent has opted out by signature at the beginning of the year. The list of students whose parents have disallowed that their children be videotaped should be accessible to you, as a teacher. Other districts have policies that forbid videotaping students in the classroom. If you work in a district such as this, you might ask the appropriate authorities if it is acceptable to capture students' voices. In such a case, you could put the recording lens on you the teacher and only capture the audio from students (of course, this can lead to confusion over who is speaking, but it can be better than nothing). Responsible practice requires that you do this investigative legwork.
- Know the policies of your school or district regarding sharing video footage of students. Again, some district policies are broadly written to allow for sharing of captured material on district websites, in district publicity materials, and in other public forums. Some schools or districts have strict policies that videotaping can be used for professional development but cannot be made available beyond that. Depending on the type of professional learning community you are a part of, you may need to secure permissions from administrators, parents, and students, to share video footage with other teachers, inside or outside the school.
- Read the fine print of any web-based or cloud-based site you use for sharing and commenting around video. For many sites, privacy is something you must pay for. Sites often claim proprietary rights and the rights to share any footage uploaded to the site; for our project, this was unacceptable.
- Use pseudonyms. Teachers in our study were required in preparing transcripts and writing about students to use pseudonyms for all students. Many even chose to use a pseudonym for the school.

While many wince at the thought of listening to their own voices, teachers we work with describe watching videorecordings of their own teaching as "eye opening" and "transformative." They report that watching themselves on video made them aware of things they were not aware of before—both positive and negative. For example, on one hand, some were surprised to learn that watching themselves actually gave them a sense of validation. In other words, because teachers are often their own harshest critics, they have a tendency to dwell on missed opportunities or missteps. Watching themselves on video sometimes reminded teachers of strengths that they had taken for granted.

On the other hand, teachers also find that video can reveal quirks and tics that they never realized they had. One new teacher we worked with noticed that he rarely strayed from the front of the room. This simple realization spurred him to use the proximity of his body to interact differently with students. Another teacher noticed that she tended to sway back and forth while she talked. She thought that habit might be distracting to students, and she easily remedied it. Finally, several teachers commented on their tendency to respond to every student turn with "okay," "good," or "mm hmm . . . " Many teachers worked to overcome that habit because they were concerned that it actually undermined their goal of encouraging students to talk to one another rather than always relying on the teacher.

## SELECT AND TRANSCRIBE A SHORT CLIP

At this point we narrow the focus even more. From the video footage you recorded, select a short clip—approximately 5 minutes—that seems particularly salient to the issue(s) you want to explore. A 5-minute clip is short enough to make the transcription and analysis manageable in terms of time and effort while also being long enough to result in valuable insight.

And then transcribe it as soon after the lesson as you reasonably can; students do not use teacher voices, and your recent memory will help you make sense of quiet or unclear contributions. The essence of transcription work looks something like this: Play the tape, type what is being said as quickly as possible, pause and rewind the tape, listen again, type some more . . . repeat. The goal is to capture to the precise words of students and yourself. Some teachers even decide to include gestures and other nonverbal aspects of classroom communication. The text box offers you pointers for transcribing.

Admittedly, teachers often express skepticism about doing such transcription. Is it worth the time and effort? You might ask, "How am I supposed to make time for transcribing classroom talk when I have lessons to plan, papers to grade, and lunch periods to supervise?" We are certainly sympathetic to the challenge of time; there is never enough. However, teachers we know—ourselves included—have so enthusiastically valued transcription (and the subsequent analysis of that transcript) that we feel confident making the bold claim that the time and effort are

---

## A Closer Look: Formatting Your Transcript

You have many options for how to format transcripts. The main issue to consider when selecting a format is one that works for you. We offer the following tips:

- Identify each student by name (or a pseudonym), rather than listing "student 1," "student 2," and so on. Having this information may be helpful as you analyze which students participate and which do not.
- Try to capture students' words as closely and completely as possible. If a word or phrase is inaudible, you can insert "[inaudible]" in its place.
- Transcribe your own words as closely and completely as possible. Your role in the discussion is of central importance.
- Make notes like "(Laughter)" or "(Many side conversations)." These kinds of contextual details can help you develop a more accurate analysis.

We have shown you examples throughout the book of transcripts made by teachers. You'll notice that some are more detailed than others, for example, including nonverbal movement and action.

---

well worth the sacrifice! In fact, many of the teachers with whom we have worked have exclaimed that it was *the single most effective assignment they encountered in a graduate methods course.* These teachers' reflections sum up what seems to be a typical perspective:

MARY BLANCA: Transcribing the footage, a task I prematurely deemed "pointless," actually helped me to catch all of the little things that were said while I was busy focusing on my next "teaching point." It only took 10 minutes and helped me to further process what my students were actually saying.

SUZANNE SCOGGINS: I particularly enjoyed the transcription. You don't really think about the little things you or your students say until you have to sit down and listen to them repeatedly as you type them out.

CAROLINE WEEKLEY: I really thought that transcribing the clip would not be a useful activity. However, I was quickly proved wrong. This truly brings a focus on just the dialogue held, and I was able to see myself, in black and white. The transcript allowed me to pay attention to every word I said, and how my students responded. It allows for a reflection upon the dialogue that is happening, since it is hard to remember everything that is said following 71 minutes of teaching, 4 times a day.

In fact, many teachers say that the act of transcription itself helped them to see themselves and their students differently from how they had before. Taking time and focusing attention to type out classroom talk word by word slows down the moment, giving teachers time to listen carefully and consider their initial perceptions differently.

## ANALYZE

Just as there are many different ways to analyze a poem, there many different ways to analyze classroom talk. When you analyze a poem, you can begin by looking for poetic devices such as simile and metaphor, figurative language, or structural elements that lead you to deeper understanding of the content of the poem. Similarly, when you analyze classroom talk, you can look for dialogic indicators such as authentic questions, teacher uptake, or participation patterns to help you evaluate whether a discussion was really dialogic. In other words, you can find many different ways in—the ways in you choose depend on what you are looking for.

For example, if you want to focus on learning more about student participation (as so many of us do), you might:

- Count the number of different students who participated and determine the percentage of people who did participate.
- Count the number of student turns (S), count the number of teacher turns (T), and determine the ratio of S:T turns.
- Examine the pattern of teacher and student talk to detect whether the discussion follows a typical IRE pattern or whether you achieved any of the desired S-S-S-S exchanges.
- Count the number of girl speakers and count the number of boy speakers to determine whether gender dynamics might be affecting participation patterns.
- Count the number of times individual students participated to determine if particular students dominated the discussion.
- Count the number of times someone responded to a previous comment.

These ideas suggest just a few of the countless ways you can gain more insight into student participation through dialogic classroom discourse analysis. In Table 6.1, we lay out dialogic indicators in a more systematic way, so you can make strategic decisions about what to look for and how to proceed with the analysis depending on your own goals and challenges.

This level of analysis is likely more fine grained than the reflection most teachers are accustomed to. Without doubt it takes time to record, transcribe, and analyze classroom interactions. This detailed level of analysis can, however, provide you with insights that you are unlikely to discover without it.

**Table 6.1. Possible "Ways in" for Dialogic Classroom Discourse Analysis**

| Question | Ways In | Analysis | Hypothetical Finding |
|---|---|---|---|
| | In the left margin of the transcript, mark "T" for each teacher turn. | Count the total number of teacher turns. Compare with the number of student turns. | If the ratio of teacher turns (T) to student turns (S) is 25:4, it suggests that the teacher is dominating the talk. |
| *How much did the teacher participate?* | Length of teacher turns | Scan the transcript to evaluate the length of teacher turns compared with the length of student turns. | If teacher turns are represented by long paragraphs and student turns are short phrases or one-word responses, it suggests that the teacher may be dominating the talk. |
| *How many students participated?* | In the left margin of the transcript, mark "S" for each student turn. Use S1, S2, S3 to indicate each different speaker. | Count the total number of student speakers and calculate the percentage of students who participated. | If 7 of 28 (25%) students participated, it suggests that the teacher might want to think about ways to generate participation from a greater number of students. |
| | Use the "Ss" in the left margin. | Count the number of times individual students participated. | If Jesse participated 33 times and all other students participated less than 3 times, it suggests that Jesse dominated the classroom talk. |
| *Which students participated?* | In the left margin, mark each student speaker as "B" for boy or "G" for girl. | Count the total number of Bs. Compare to the total number of Gs. | If 17 of the student speakers were boys and 4 of the student speakers were girls, it suggests that boys may be dominating the classroom talk. |
| *What were the participation patterns?* | T-S-T-S or T-S-S-S | Look at the pattern of Ts and Ss down the left margin. | If the pattern looks like T-S-T-S-T, it fits a typical IRE recitation pattern and the teacher might want to think about how to achieve more of an S-S-S pattern. |

*(continued)*

95

Table 6.1. *(continued)*

| Question | Ways In | Analysis | Hypothetical Finding |
|---|---|---|---|
| | In the right margin, mark "TAQ" for each Teacher Authentic Question. | Count the total number of TAQs. Or count how many different students responded to a single TAQ. Or analyze the quality of the questions you asked. | TAQs are generally recognized as being positive indicators of dialogic teaching. |
| | In the right column, mark "TNQ" for each Teacher Nonauthentic Question. | Count the total number of TNQs. Also, examine the nature of student responses to TNQ. | TNQs are often an indicator of classroom talk that is more display-driven. If students responded with surface-level, text-based answers to TNQs, the teacher might want to think about asking more TAQs. |
| *How did the teacher participate?* | In the right column, mark "TU" for each time you demonstrate uptake. | Count the number of TUs. | TU is a sign that the teacher is responding to what the students have said. If uptake is rare, the teacher might want to think about ways to be more responsive to students' contributions. |
| | In the right column, mark "R" for each instance of revoicing. | Count the number of Rs. Or, look at the nature of the Rs. | Sometimes teachers revoice students' responses in ways that perpetuate the typical IRE pattern. Other times, teachers use revoicing in combination with an extending question as an uptake technique. |
| | In the right column, mark "CM" for each instance of Classroom Management. | Count the number of CMs. Analyze the nature of the CMs. | If there is a high number of CMs, the teacher might want to think about different ways of configuring student talk or consider designing a meta-lesson about norms and expectations. |

| | | | |
|---|---|---|---|
| | Length | Scan the transcript to evaluate the length of student turns. | If students respond with one-word answers or short phrases, the teacher may want to think about ways to solicit more substantial responses from students. |
| | In the right margin, mark "SQ" for each student-generated question. | Count the number of student-generated questions. | Student questions are generally recognized as a positive sign of dialogic interaction.<br>If SQs are rare, the teacher might want to think about using a tool designed to generate student questions. |
| *How did students participate?* | In the right column, mark "SU" for each time a student demonstrates uptake, or responds to what another student says. | Count the number of SUs. | SU signals that students are responding to what other students have said. If uptake rarely happens among students, the teacher might want to think about ways to teach students to attune more to one another's contributions. |

## REVISE YOUR PRACTICE

The real value of dialogic discourse analysis rests on the extent to which analyses actually improve the quality of talk in the classroom. As we mentioned early on in this chapter, teachers can use dialogic classroom discourse analysis as a tool for troubleshooting the challenges they face in their classroom and also for recognizing problems they didn't even know existed. To that end, you might follow your analysis with reflective questions such as

- What patterns or "problems" did the analysis reveal?
- What insights came from the dialogic classroom discourse analysis?
- What would be some logical teaching strategies that might grow out of those insights?
- How might specific dialogic tools help me respond to challenges?

## VIGNETTE 1: MADELYN

Madelyn, an early career teacher, taught in a school district with a prescribed curriculum. With prepackaged lesson plans that scripted much of her class time, Madelyn struggled to find opportunities to integrate meaningful whole-group discussion. Invested in the potential of dialogic instruction, she was determined not only to make opportunities for talk but also to make the most of those opportunities when they arose. Madelyn wanted to work on pushing the conversation to the next level. She noticed that her students often responded with short and surface-level comments. She hoped to gain more insight into the role she could play in generating more substantial responses.

Madelyn recorded herself and her students during her British literature course. After getting over the jitters of recording herself the first time, she actually found the videorecording to be a very helpful tool all on its own. In fact, she started to record and watch herself frequently. She reflected;

> The whole process of videotaping myself has been really interesting. I do it almost every day. I just use my laptop camera. . . . It has really helped me to speak with more purpose and sound more professional. It has also helped me go back and reflect on how I could have said things differently or how I could have held my body differently. I noticed that I flipped/flicked my hands when I asked Nick to be quiet, and that motion really gets on my nerves watching it again. The camera has also helped me with classroom management. Sometimes I point [the camera] just at the students and then later I watch it and I've seen a lot of things through the video that I never saw a hint of during class time. Even though I don't so much love looking at myself on video, I realize that it is extremely helpful.

She decided to take a closer look at a clip from a whole-group discussion about *Frankenstein*, by Mary Shelley. She selected a clip from a discussion that took place about two-thirds of the way through the novel unit, in which she asked students to consider Victor's responsibility for the creature's actions. Before jumping into the whole-group discussion, she had asked students to develop their ideas in writing, using two quotes from the text to substantiate their arguments. Madelyn felt that this discussion would be rich for dialogic discourse analysis, because students had had a chance to process their thinking in writing beforehand and because the prompt required students to demonstrate higher-order thinking skills. At the same time, this was exactly the kind of discussion that she had struggled with in the past. She hoped to find out why.

Madelyn began by exploring the participation pattern by marking teacher turns (T) and student turns (S) in the left-hand margin of her transcript, as the text box below illustrates. She was disappointed to find that this discussion fit the typical IRE pattern. Determined to interrupt this pattern, Madelyn went on to analyze the nature of her own turns: "Of the 25 times I spoke, 10 of those times were validating or recognizing the student spoke with 'okay' or 'mm hmm,' or 'good.'" She did not feel that these turns contributed much to the discussion. Based on her analysis of this transcript, she was able to identify these types of turns as ones that could be avoided in the future to create more opportunities for students to respond to one another.

Because Madelyn wanted to increase student participation, she counted the number of student speakers by marking S1, S2, S3, S4 (Student 1, Student 2, Student 3, Student 4) in the left-hand margin. She noted: "Of 28 students who were present in class that day, only 7 talked." Overall, the percentage disappointed her.

Upon closer inspection, Madelyn noticed that gender also played a role in the discussion. Boys participated more than girls in her class:

> One of the major disappointments for me was who participated and who didn't. I had only seven speakers: five boys and two girls. The boys spoke 22 times, and the girls spoke 7 times. Before class even started I spoke with a girl who had some really great insight into the book, but she didn't speak once during the entire conversation. I hadn't realized how much I didn't hear from her and others like her.

Madelyn vowed to pay attention to gender in future discussions.

In addition to counting the total number of student speakers, Madelyn paid attention to who those speakers were: "Nate spoke four times, Nick spoke once, Christian spoke five times, Paul spoke five times, Mike spoke seven times, Natalie spoke six times, and Grace spoke once." She went on to think about what that meant: "I don't believe the other 21 students in class weren't engaged (although a few weren't). I believe that my talkers are the most outgoing students and simply dominated."

## Madelyn's Annotated Transcript

S1   **Natalie:** Well, the monster says, "Do your duty towards me," uh, right, and, "and I will do mine towards you and the rest of mankind." So he kinda, the monster kinda says, like, I won't do bad things either if you help me out, kinda.

T   **Teacher:** Emmm hmm.

S1   **Natalie:** So he's kind of taking responsibility for killing all the people, I don't know.

T   **Teacher:** I don't know.

S2   **Nick:** I'll read mine. Alright, um, "Yet you my creator detest and spurn me thy creature to whom thou are bound by ties only dissoluble only by annihilation by one of us" and that all means that, um, the monster knows that the creator doesn't like him and he doesn't feel responsible, but he is.

T   **Teacher:** Okay.

S3   **Nate:** I think he's responsible because he created it and it started the whole mess so that's why I think he's responsible for it. If he wouldn't have created it, none of it would have ever happened.

S4   **Paul:** I don't know if this is right, but, um, Frankenstein kinda says, "I will leave them and you at peace but if you refuse I will . . . the something of death until it be stated with blood of your remaining friends." So like he's kinda saying he could just go out and slaughter everybody and not even care what Victor's saying but instead he kind of offers him up like a one or the other situation . . . like, he's still offering peace with him and stuff, when he could go rage and kill them.

T   **Teacher:** Mmm hmm.

S5   **Chris:** I found one where it showed Victor like not taking personal responsibility.

T   **Teacher:** Oh, great!

S5   **Chris:** In part of it he says, "Begone, I will not hear you."

T   **Teacher:** Okay.

S5   **Chris:** Kinda saying as, "I don't want you here. I don't want to listen to anything that you are saying so you better just leave."

T   **Teacher:** Okay, so he's shunning his responsibility, right? "I'm not going to be responsible, I want you out of here." R

S5   **Chris:** Which he should have more responsibility for it because he created it and if he would have stayed with the creature then he could have taught it right from wrong and now it kind of seems like the creature doesn't know.

T   **Teacher:** Right, but we can see that the creature is capable of learning, right? TU/TNQ

S3   **Nate:** When you look at both of those quotes, the creature says, "Stay here and talk to me or I'm going to go kill people," and then he says, "Leave." So he's kind of just saying, "Go kill more people." He doesn't want the creature to be his problem.

T   **Teacher:** What's the, um, which one of those quotes comes first? Do you guys know? Can anybody find it? TU/TAQ

S3   **Nate:** That one.

S1   **Natalie:** Ummm, I think that one, right?

T   **Teacher:** The "go away?"

S1   **Natalie:** Yeah.

S3   **Nate:** I think he's telling him to go away after that.

T   **Teacher:** I think he says, "Listen to me," and he's like, "No, just leave," and then "Listen to me, listen to me, listen to me." He has to tell him a couple of times. Does anybody agree with that? Or am I wrong? TAQ

S5   **Chris:** "Be gone once" is on page 22 in the school book.

T   **Teacher:** Okay.

S1   **Natalie:** I don't think it's fully Frankenstein's thing because responsibility is about making choices and the monster is like giving him a choice kinda, like, "I'll do this or this depending on what you do," so that means the monster is capable of being responsible. Right?

S6   **Grace:** The monster stays out like 4 nights in the wilderness. He was responsible enough to take care of himself.

Finally, Madelyn wondered about the quality of her own participation in the discussion, so she looked for teacher authentic questions (TAQs), teacher uptake (TU), and revoicing (R), which she marked after completed turns. She learned that

> of the 15 questions I asked, only 10 were authentic and 5 were not. I wondered if using uptake led to more authentic questions, but it was split evenly. Of the four times I used uptake, two led to authentic questions and two led to nonauthentic questions. Analyzing the transcript helped me understand that I can ask more authentic questions. I think I can use uptake to ask more authentic questions.

Madelyn wanted to up the ante on the level of thinking taking place during discussion. She wanted students not only to speak in extended turns but also to achieve higher levels of critical thinking in those responses. As she explored their individual contributions, she reflected:

> Their responses during this time were pretty good. I asked students to respond to the theme of responsibility and to find quotes to support their assertions. Because students had [written in response to the prompt] before we sat down to discuss, I think the discussion consisted of productive and helpful conversations. However, the flipside to that is that I think students focused on contributing their ideas regarding responsibility and not always about building off of what their classmates said.

As is often the case, as soon as Madelyn began to reflect on the analysis, she generated several ideas for next steps like focusing on asking more authentic questions and avoiding "validating" comments, such as "Mmmm hmmm" and "Good," after every student turn. She planned to plan ways to include more student voices next time. Specifically, she thought dialogic tools, such as think-pair-shares and small groups might generate participation from more students. She also identified new goals for her students, in terms of learning to listen to one another and building their comments on each others' ideas in cumulative talk.

## VIGNETTE 2: KRISTA

Krista, also an early career teacher, taught in a racially, culturally, economically, and linguistically diverse urban school for the arts. Her 10th-graders, who were more accustomed to teacher-centered classroom talk, had little experience with student-centered dialogic interactions. As a result, Krista found that her students often talked over one another and formulated their own responses without really listening to one another. She was frustrated that her own participation in the discussion entailed mostly classroom management. Krista and her students had been working on holding more independent discussions for a semester. Krista had been gradually releasing more and more responsibility over to her students. Had her students made progress toward more independent discussions? She wanted to take a closer look.

She decided to videorecord a whole-group discussion that took place during their study of *The Great Gatsby*. She reflected:

> At first, I was really dreading this project. I didn't want to videotape myself. How embarrassing! When I came home and watched myself, it was interesting. I learned what the students see and hear when I'm leading a class. I felt like I was constantly yelling at them. How I project my voice is something I'm going to be conscious of from now on. It was also interesting to see what my students were doing from the opposite side of the room. It's hard to see everything from the front of the class, especially when I'm calling on people, trying to listen to what they're saying, and then writing it on the board. It's hard to watch yourself and see all the things you do not like about how you teach. It was definitely eye-opening. I learned a lot from doing this. I was able to look at myself and find things I would change or do better.

Getting her students to talk was not the challenge; getting them to listen to one another and build their responses off of each other's ideas was her challenge. So, to focus her dialogic discourse analysis, Krista zeroed in on their use of an anticipation guide she designed to activate prior knowledge before reading the novel. The anticipation guide was designed to pique students' interest in themes of the novel and invite them to speak from their own experiences, and Krista expected that students would have a lot to say. At the same time, these kinds of high-participation discussions were exactly the kind of discussions that had presented challenges in the past. She hoped a closer examination of a classroom interaction would shed some light on how to go about it differently in the future.

Krista began her analysis by counting the number of turns she took during their discussion, marking teacher turns (T) in the left-hand margin, illustrated in the text box below. She found that

> there were a total of 83 comments in my 5-minute clip. Out of those 83 comments, 31 of the comments were mine. I thought talking two-fifths of the time was not so awful. It was definitely an improvement from my previous discussions.

She proceeded to examine the nature of her own participation. She noticed that many of her turns were devoted to "classroom management":

> Of the 31 times I talked, 9 of my comments were to correct behavior, which was not a surprise. Since my students are still getting used to this whole dialogic discussion idea, they often get excited and talk over each other. I

### Krista's Annotated Manuscript

T    **Teacher:** Pay attention. If you truly love another person long enough, you will eventually have a life together. TAQ/BM

S    **Class:** Yes! Agree . . . Agree . . . I agree . . .

T    **Teacher:** Okay, one at a time! One at a time. Who wants to go first? TM/BM

S1   **James:** What'd you say?

T    **Teacher:** All right, let's start with Randi, then go around and we can all have a comment. Randi? TM

S2   **Randi:** I disagree because basically you can love another person, but they love somebody else.

S1   **James:** I agree and disagree.

T    **Teacher:** All right, why? TU/TAQ

S3   **Kobe:** I agree because if you love somebody then . . . pause . . . I disagree because what Randi said or you, you could love somebody for a long time, but then you can fall out of love with them.

T    **Teacher:** Okay . . . all right. Juan, what were you gonna say? Shh! Juan, what where you gonna say? TM/BM

S4   **Juan:** I do not agree to this reason because if you love someone, that other person might not have the same feelings. They might be into someone else that they see or more. They might not want you, but the other person does.

T    **Teacher:** Okay, so same kind of similar thing, right? You can be in love with someone, but they might not love you back. R

S5   **Kelly:** I agree. [Raises hand.] I agree because if you love somebody, he supposed to love you back . . . or she.

S6   **Jonah:** Right, why you gonna love somebody, who don't love you?

S1   **James:** Yah!

S    **Class:** For real. Right?

T    **Teacher:** All right. Geoff? TM

S7   **Geoff:** I agree because there's people in the world that have loved each other since high school and they married and they still together.

S1   **James:** Like my momma and daddy's school, they went to the same school and they still married.

T    **Teacher:** But what if you love that person and they don't love you back? Are you still eventually gonna have a life together? TU/TAQ

S    **Class:** [Lots of comments . . . inaudible.]

T    **Teacher:** Shh . . . all right! All right! We gotta hear each other. We gotta hear each other. BM

S6   **Jonah:** Then you leave 'em and just move on to the next one.

T    **Teacher:** All right . . .

S4   **Juan:** Wait a minute . . .

T    **Teacher:** So you disagree then, you don't think you'll eventually have a life together? TU/TAQ

S    **Class:** [Talking . . . inaudible.]

S1   **James:** That's so bad . . .

S6   **Jonah:** Well, they would if that person loves you . . . I mean . . . but if they don't love you, you just move on.

T    **Teacher:** All right. Over here, what were you gonna say, Kelly? TM

S4   **Juan:** How you gonna love . . . how you gonna love somebody, if they don't love you back?

*(continued)*

---

**Krista's Annotated Manuscript** *(continued)*

S2  **Randi:** That's the whole point of love songs . . .
S8  **Kelly:** 'Cause they care about you.
S6  **Jonah:** Well then, man, you too obsessed with them . . .
S8  **Kelly:** [Inaudible side comment.]
T   **Teacher:** All right. Krystal, what do you think? Tell us your comment. What do you think? Do you think if you love 'em long enough, you'll eventually have a life together? TAQ
S1  **James:** Krystal ain't sayin' nothing.
T   **Teacher:** Shh . . . just agree or disagree. BM/TM
S9  **Krystal:** I disagree.
T   **Teacher:** Disagree? R
S9  **Krystal:** [Nods.]
T   **Teacher:** All right. Anyone else? What do you guys think? We haven't heard from some people. TM/TAQ
S1  **James:** [Inaudible side comment.]
T   **Teacher:** Someone who hasn't talked. Give us your opinion. What do you think? Shh . . . TM/BM

---

begin to feel threatened when I think students are all talking at once and not hearing each other. I wonder if all my behavior corrections were necessary or me overreacting to what I perceived as chaos.

She noticed another pattern in her turns, which was related to the way she facilitated turn taking. She began calling these turns "teacher moves," which she marked with "TM" in the transcript.

Another 9 comments were teacher moves. The teacher moves are where I'm structuring the discussion, either calling on people or establishing the rotation of who is going to talk. Only a few times do I uptake and push my students further. This would be a good place to start letting my students take over.

Next, she counted the number of students who participated by marking student turns (S1, S2, S3 . . . ) in the left-hand margin. This line of analysis helped her to realize that "of 14 people in class, I had a total of 11 people participate. I thought this was a pretty good number." A closer look at student participation indicated to her that they were, in fact, making progress toward her goal of engaging more students in discussion.

Finally, she explored the nature of students' participation:

The only problem was they don't usually listen to each other or answer each other; they are just stating their opinions out loud. So although in the discussion transcript it looks good that so many students were talking, I'm not sure if how they were doing it ended up being beneficial to the discussion.

Based on her analysis of the 5-minute transcript, Krista decided that it might be helpful to have a meta-discussion to review the rules of effective discussion. For example, she wanted to emphasize the importance of waiting until a speaker has spoken before raising a hand to speak. She even speculated about showing students clips of the discussion video to invite them into the process of assessing how they are doing as discussion participants. She also considered using some kind of pass toy (see Table 3.2) that students could pass around to emphasize the importance of taking turns. In all these ways, Krista planned to continue working toward helping her students be more self-sufficient in whole-group discussions.

Dialogic classroom discourse analysis is not meant to be rigid or lockstep. It is a recursive process that can lead not only to revising your practice but also to new questions, challenges, and goals. We encourage you to move through and/or repeat the steps we have described at a pace that is useful to you. In the next chapter, we suggest ways to bring colleagues into the process.

# CHAPTER 7

# Transforming Practice Through Collegial Collaboration

Through reading this book, you've become acquainted with a rationale for adopting dialogic teaching and doing it now; you've learned the lingo of dialogic teaching; you may have planned for dialogic learning talk at the day-to-day, unit, or yearlong level; you've tackled some of the challenges that naturally arise with dialogic teaching; you've explored using dialogic teaching in literature and writing instruction; and you've started to analyze your own practice using discourse analysis. Now what?

Find others who are doing the same.

This chapter invites you into the practice of reviewing dialogic practice within a professional learning community. It's only logical: To figure out how talk is going in your classroom, talk about it with others who talk the dialogic talk you do.

## A PROFESSIONAL LEARNING COMMUNITY IN ACTION

Meet Maricela Reimann, Melissa Sherr, Slater Seybert, Carmella Brasfeld, and Rachael Hughes. These new teachers chose to work together in a professional learning community (PLC) with a focus on dialogic teaching over the course of the school year. Some members of the group were in urban schools, others suburban. Some were in English classrooms, others ESL. Some were in high school, others middle school.

Their PLC met both online and in person. They used online platforms to share video clips of their own teaching. Then, colleagues commented on the video through typed text, oral recordings, or short videos. Their online discussion was generally followed by face-to-face conversations when they met in their English methods courses the following week or month. For specific details regarding technology and logistics, please visit our website (vbrr.wiki.educ.msu.edu).

Let's take a look at this PLC's work together. In this instance, Melissa recorded and posted a clip to her group's online platform in January, about halfway through

## A Closer Look: Professional Learning Communities in an English Methods Course

Video and Internet technologies have made it easier to document and share classroom interactions. Digital video facilitates recording, reviewing, and representing teaching and learning in various contexts, and the Internet makes it possible for digital videos to be shared online, along with other classroom discourse artifacts like lesson plans, syllabi, and student work. Digital video, the Internet, and web-based social networking capabilities thus provide tools for teachers to access multiple examples of classroom interactions across a variety of classroom contexts (Hatch & Pointer-Mace, 2007; Jenkins, 2006).

Inspired by how digitally mediated review and response work could support early career teachers working to develop dialogic teaching talk and student learning talk into their practice, our author team designed and researched PLCs centered around dialogic teaching. We required students to form into PLCs as part of the English methods master's curriculum at our university. (For more detail, see Heintz, Borsheim, Caughlan, Juzwik, & Sherry, 2010; Juzwik, Sherry, Caughlan, Heintz, & Borsheim-Black, 2012.)

the school year. In her introductory remarks prefacing the clip, Melissa expresses a concern about the lesson she's teaching in the clip, wondering if it is "dialogic enough." She asked her colleagues for feedback. Maricela was the first to respond, also via their online platform: "Nice wait time throughout this recitation. You give them a moment to process and think about the questions without making that silence feel awkward or too long." Maricela identifies the type of instructional practice Melissa uses—recitation—and judges that Melissa is making use of time to make space for student voices within that recitation. Maricela points out that dialogic techniques are being employed in a recitation, a type of instructional practice not typically associated with dialogic teaching. Slater weighs in:

> I agree with Maricela; in this video you did do a lot of leading of the discussion, but it is supposed to be a college-level class designed to prepare them for college where they will encounter more discussions like this rather than a "fishbowl" activity. It's more of a real-world experience for them, so I think it was fine. If you're concerned that this wasn't dialogic enough you could have students sign up to lead the discussions so that it is more student driven. Of course, that comes with its own risks too. I would say great job overall and don't worry if sometimes your classroom looks more traditional.

Slater agrees with Maricela's assessment, adds some reasoning behind why this claim is valid (preparation for college), and offers an extension to the lesson—inviting students to sign up to lead a discussion. Both Maricela and Slater offer Melissa some moral support. Carmella joins the conversation:

> I agree with both Slater and Maricela. I think that teaching in this style every now and then is probably beneficial to an extent since these are AP students who obviously enjoy the subject of English (or can at least perform well enough to be in an AP class) and have the capacity to follow along. As Slater stated, this is the style of teaching they are going to be faced with in most college classrooms so it's a good experience for them to learn how to operate in it now. I also like Maricela's idea about assigning student leaders for discussion. I know that this group of kids usually participates a lot more and does take over the discussion more than can be seen in this footage; however, it may be interesting to have them do "teacher for a day" assignments where they are in charge of dissecting a piece and leading the class in doing the same. This would definitely prepare them for doing it on their own in the exam.

By the time this conversation took place, the group had already worked together as a PLC for a full semester. During that time, they had shared stories about their classrooms as well as two video clips. In commenting, Carmella thus had more contextual knowledge of her colleague's classroom than this clip on its own can represent. This contextual knowledge enabled her to suggest an extension or revision to Melissa's practice that she knows is feasible, given her understanding of Melissa's population of students. Rachael, the fourth member in Melissa's group, chimes in:

> At the beginning of the class, you were sure to activate prior knowledge by mentioning the last discussion/reading. Good, lol. It seems like most of the students are paying attention and I heard a lot of different voices . . . perhaps even 50%!

As we learned in Chapter 6, it is important to consider not only how often students participated but also how often various students in a classroom participated. Some teacher transcripts (see Chapter 6) would at first glance look promising in terms of dialogic student participation (e.g., teacher turns would be followed in most every case by student turns). But a closer look would reveal that 1 or 2 students were speaking in each of those student turns, while the other 30 students did not say anything. Rachael points out how many students contribute within just 5 minutes in Melissa's class.

So, what did Melissa gain as a result of sharing her dialogic practice with her colleagues?

- She got feedback on a lingering question about her work taking a dialogic stance.
- She got validation in her use of wait time, her activation of prior knowledge, and her soliciting of multiple student voices.
- She got a consensus of opinion on making the recitation a task or assignment that students themselves could take on, along with a rationale for this suggested task. This rationale included both its potential for future application and its current appropriateness given her student group.

## DIALOGIC RESPONSE TO
## DIALOGIC PRACTICE

Just as dialogic teaching encourages knowledge building via the clash, crescendo, and consensus of many voices, dialogic review and response encourage new understanding of one's own practice. Unlike a boilerplate tick-the-boxes evaluation of practice, dialogic response encourages each teacher to think of each video clip as simply a draft in an ongoing teaching practice. While some teacher growth will result simply via the process of making a video, selecting a clip, contextualizing it, and reviewing it, we find evidence from groups like Melissa's that new and enlightened thinking about practice grew out of dialogue with other teachers. The video captures what happened in the classroom, warts and all. The dialogue around the video describes, tests, and evaluates what happened, and imagines beyond it, all to prepare the teacher for another class period—another draft in an ongoing manuscript of teaching. Dialogic review and response can be a kind of "time outside of time" that gives teachers space outside the classroom to brainstorm and develop better practices for when they re-enter the classroom. It allows teachers to put each day's practice into conversation with their practices of the past and their ambitions for the future.

Another benefit of dialogic review and response is that each of the reviewers in Melissa's group was able to take in the feedback of all colleagues and apply it to their own practice as well. In the case of the dialogue around Melissa's practice, the concepts of wait time, activating prior knowledge, soliciting multiple student voices, and taking a dialogic stance within a recitation were raised for all group members to consider with respect to their own practice. These particular concepts may not have been raised in response to each of the teachers' videos. However, being part of a PLC, in which comments to one teacher are viewable by all other teachers, ensures that as a member of a community you have access to wider (and perhaps less personally threatening) conversations around dialogic practice than if you were only seeing/hearing comments on your own practice.

Now that you have seen the potential in the process through an example case, here are some steps toward organizing your own PLC.

## PUTTING TOGETHER YOUR OWN
## DIALOGIC PLC AROUND DIALOGIC PRACTICE

### Assemble a Group

Maybe you're already part of a PLC, or maybe you meet regularly with your subject or grade-level colleagues and you'd like to try to make dialogic teaching a focus of your shared inquiry. Maybe you would rather pursue this review of your teaching with teacher friends in another school, city, or state. We offer a few tips for assembling your review and response group around dialogic teaching.

*If Possible, Self-Select a Group.* Opening your practice up to others is not an easy task. If there is a group of people with whom you already feel comfortable, you might consider working with them. Or you might organize around a common interest or area of expertise. For example, the members of one group with whom we worked got together around their shared focus on ESL. Whether your comfort level with a colleague is based on shared content area, multiple years working together, or just "that person gets you," trust matters. Trust becomes especially important for giving and receiving feedback beyond "That was great!" In our experience, group members need to trust each other enough to provide honest critique and thoughtful suggestions.

*If Possible, Work in Heterogeneous Groups.* The teachers with whom we worked were all first-year teachers (for more detail about our research project, see Appendix B). Many likened their collaboration to the blind leading the blind. If you are able, you might find it beneficial to work with teachers who are different from you in key ways. For example, you might learn a lot from teachers with more experience teaching, with more expertise working with digital technologies, with strong classroom management skills or with expertise in other content areas. Putting together a group may be a balance of finding those you are comfortable with, those who will help you stretch, and those willing to commit the time and energy to regular, reflective practice.

*Determine the Size and Nature of the Group.* Another element to consider is whether you'd like to be part of a community that has a broad, shifting membership or part of a more close-knit group. Falk and Drayton (2009) outline two different types of online communities:

- Community forums: long-running electronic communities that have a broad, growing, and shifting membership base
- Communities interacting in targeted professional learning environments: communities that engage smaller populations for a more well-defined period

The teachers with whom we worked organized into smaller PLCs (four to five teachers each) for a well-defined period (one school year) and they met both online and in person. You may prefer a face-to-face group, which can facilitate more immediate feedback. Or you may prefer to collaborate online with colleagues outside your school or community.

## Discuss Your Focus

This book is designed to support an in-depth inquiry into teaching and learning talk. You might begin by reading chapters of this book, setting goals for dialogic instruction, and mobilizing different dialogic tools in your classroom. As you and your colleagues work together, you may become more fluent in the language of dialogic instruction, using terms like *uptake*, *wait time*, *authentic questions*, and so on. You and your group might take advantage of our additional resources, such as the reproducibles found on our website (vbrr.wiki.educ.msu.edu).

## Assemble the Tools

If the members in your PLC all teach at the same school, you may need to book a place to meet, arrange to use school technological equipment (such as cameras and laptops), and decide on an online platform to share. You may decide you want to conduct your collaborative review practice entirely online, in which case, each member would be responsible for securing his or her own recording equipment, and choice of a shared online platform becomes supremely important. The web-based tools you would need to conduct such an inquiry may be freely available to you. We offer more specific information about current tools and resources on our website (vbrr.wiki.educ.msu.edu).

## Set Goals but Remain Flexible

How long will this sustained inquiry last? How much time will you allow for between posting and reviewing? How many posts do you hope to contribute and discuss within a month/a semester/a year? Your goal may be to do a slow roll out of dialogic teaching over the course of a school year. It may be to make a particularly thorny unit for you in terms of student participation, such as test prep, more active for your students. Your (and your colleagues') goals for your work in terms of time may help to dictate how often you videotape, how often the videotape is made available for a dialogic conversation, and so on.

Consider building in a pilot stage. Teachers we worked with found they had a lot of kinks to work out. Before committing to a particular technology, timeline, and so on, give yourself a trial period, after which you'll revisit to revise not only your *teaching* practice but also your *collaborative* practice as a professional learning community.

## Experiment with Ways of Communicating

Try not to make *all* the dialogue around video clips asynchronous and online. The teachers with whom we worked posted their clips, watched each other's clips, and responded to each other—all online. While the specific feedback they received online was useful, they also valued opportunities to discuss their videos and responses in real time and in person. A synchronous, real-time meeting has the potential to better capitalize on the back-and-forth of a group dynamic. Some online tools (e.g., Google Hangouts) can support such an experience virtually.

## Set Up Accountability

Collaboration works best if it is regular and rigorous. You may find that you can build accountability into your group using other professional expectations: for example, preparing materials for an annual review. This collaborative inquiry process can help toward that end.

## SHARING YOUR PRACTICE

## Share a Video Clip

A video clip offers an artifact that you and your colleagues can collaborate around. We have discovered that video can be invaluable because it allows your colleagues to see what actually happened in the classroom. If you simply describe a classroom interaction, you do so from your own perspective and from the point of view of retrospecting and remembering. The video footage, on the other hand, allows colleagues to see classroom practice as it happened and potentially from a point of view other than yours. In other words, the video allows for a more direct presentation of teaching practice without having to rely only on your memory.

## Provide Context

You may be more likely to get the feedback you desire if you offer your colleagues a little direction. So you might begin by asking members of your PLC to focus their attention on a specific challenge you experienced or a technique you are working on. Sisk-Hilton (2009) refers to this direction as "consultancy," when you pose a particular question for your colleagues to address. Offering this direction might also make your colleagues feel comfortable giving feedback, without feeling fearful of being too direct or critical.

Providing additional, contextualizing information for your colleagues may also ensure that they are able to give you their most useful feedback. For example, you might include your lesson plan, learning objectives, assessments, or handouts.

Some teachers with whom we have worked also found it useful to have a transcript of that clip in front of them as they watched the clip, as it may be difficult to understand student voices. Your colleagues can refer back to the lesson plans if they have questions.

## Build on Feedback

Throughout this book we have compared teaching with drafting and revising writing. Ultimately it is your choice whether you take your colleagues' advice or not, but the ultimate goal is to revise that first draft and to build the habit of continually refining and reflecting on your practice.

## Repeat

This process is not meant to be rigid or lockstep. We encourage you to move through or repeat the steps at a pace that is useful to you, with more or less time given at particular phases until you gain insight into your particular questions and challenges. Often the reflection and revision leads naturally to continued focus on growth toward the original area of focus. Or the process can lead teachers to discover new questions, challenges, and goals to work toward.

## ANOTHER PROFESSIONAL LEARNING COMMUNITY IN ACTION

Libby Ancheta, who we introduced in Chapter 5, videotaped and shared with her PLC colleagues two different tries at running a Socratic seminar. Recall that Libby invited students to participate in the seminar as preparation for writing an argumentative position paper on capital punishment with her 10th-graders. She did this lesson in the fall with one group of students and then again in the spring with a new group of students.

Libby did not receive much feedback on her fall post from her PLC. Early on in their first year of teaching and in their first meetings together as a group, she and her colleagues were tentative about offering constructive criticism. It took them a few months to get in the regular swing of viewing and responding, along with everything else they were facing as new teachers. As we will see, their feedback became more productive as they continued to work together over the course of the year.

Libby reflected on her own practice in the fall: "A particularly successful moment for me was when I saw students 'uptaking.' To me when a student is able to see a topic from the other side's perspective, they are thinking about the topic critically. That is the goal of my instruction!" Libby identifies what counts for her as quality participation (see Chapter 6)—in this case, being able to see a topic from the other side's perspective—and cites it as a goal for discussions in her classroom. She also wonders about her role within the discussion.

When she teaches this lesson again in the spring, she shifts her role in the discussion: She involves herself more by calling on students and "directing traffic." If we compare portions of her fall and spring transcripts, we also see Libby becoming more effective at managing back chatter.

In her fall post, Libby says, "*Shh*. Can you guys hear?" In her spring post, Libby more boldly directs, manages, comments on, and guides the discussion:

> TEACHER: Okay, hold on let's quiet down a little because Cecilia has
>     something to say, so let's be quiet so we can hear.
> [Silence.]
> TEACHER: Okay, let's hear from this side over here; do you have anything to
>     say?

Rather than Libby just asking for quiet, her later transcript shows her expressing why speaking over another hurts the *quality of the talk* and takes away from the learning possible during the seminar.

Libby's colleagues posted the following comments on her clip of the revised Socratic seminar:

> LARA: Hi, Libby, from the video, it looks like the majority of your students
>     are engaged. They are listening to their classmates, and when they get
>     off track, you successfully bring them back. I think this video shows the
>     sophistication of your students' ability to use discussion purposefully.
>     They don't wait for you to draw elaborated responses from them;
>     they challenge each other to do this. You have obviously provided the
>     scaffolding necessary for your students to use uptake; essentially they
>     are the center of the classroom, as evidenced by them being the focal
>     point of the video.

> FRANZ: I like how you are trying different classroom setups for discussion.
>     It shows a real effort to experiment and find what works best. I noticed
>     you are very out of the discussion, stepping in only when things get a
>     little out of hand; you're really getting good at these dialogues. I think
>     it's a good thing that you're giving the students some room to throw
>     their weight around. If you feel the need to improve, perhaps you
>     could work on the students regulating themselves and being better
>     listeners. You know what I mean? You've gotten to where you can have
>     a discussion free of you, the teacher, so now it's just about fine-tuning
>     the students' abilities to successfully discuss. Based on how involved the
>     students are, I would say you picked a good, authentic question/topic
>     for them to explore. Overall, you are really nailing this discussion stuff. I
>     found myself wanting to give my input too!

OLIVER: Libby, so you are trying to use the Socratic seminar guidelines for this discussion? Did you let them start out, possibly before this clip, just talking without you calling on people? Did this prove to be too loud and chaotic so you chose to call on them? Honestly, I think you have to call on people to talk, at this age. It was hard, even in our Friday classes, to get a word in edgewise in the Socratic circle, so I think it is necessary that you control this conversation a little. Also there is a little bit of disruption after someone comments, and before the next person comments, and I realize that this is just students being a little "squirrelly" but it makes the discussion hard to hear. You need to be on top of this, and you are. I notice a girl holding up another girl's hand . . . what's going on here? Since I have 6th-graders, I would definitely be all over that, what with students not supposed to be touching one another. She's getting ignored for the first third of the clip. Did you notice this? I like that this conversation eventually turns toward the text you just read. Sometimes, when you have students making scenarios about moral issues, like death and murder, things seem to get a little muddled. I would have liked to hear more students refer to things that happened in your reading.

You may notice that Libby's colleagues aren't afraid to be critical of her practice. By this spring post, members of the PLC freely speak their minds, and Libby sees the effects of continual response and revision. Both factors speak to the benefits of making subtle adjustments and opening up practice to a group of colleagues over many months. Libby notes in the spring:

This is the second time I taught this exact class, but an entire new group of students. I really tried to take what I learned the first time around to assess myself as a teacher and students as learners, so that I could make this a better learning experience. Prior to the video I gave them a Socratic seminar outline that set up the expectations. I have to tell you that I am very proud of this discussion. I saw my kids making connections to what we were studying and also thinking critically about the topic and uptaking by responding to each other. I was so proud of them.

Your group will review what you give them to work with. You might think about ways to intentionally use your group's feedback to improve your teaching, one draft at a time.

# Troubleshooting Common Challenges

It is very easy to talk about dialogic teaching in theory. It is not always so easy to pull it off in practice. In fact, we are well aware that discussions do not always go as smoothly in the classroom as they do in the examples presented in this book. And getting students to talk is not the only challenge. Managing what happens when they do talk can present different challenges. Because the inner workings of effective discussions are often invisible or taken for granted, you may feel surprised or disappointed when your own discussions do not go as smoothly as planned. Students may distract one another with side conversations. They may offer superficial responses. They may say things that are offensive to other students. Or they may disagree and spark heated disagreements.

If (or when) these things happen, you may decide that whole-group dialogic interactions are not for you. You may decide that you are just not good at facilitating discussion. You may shy away from trying again or decide against discussion altogether. The truth is that, as introduced in Chapter 1, dialogic interactions can present challenges for all teachers—new and veteran. This Coda offers examples of the kinds of challenges that might arise when you offer space for student talk. Thinking through challenges that other teachers have faced can support you in thinking about what you could do, what you should do, or what you should not do if you find yourself in similar circumstances. Each section offers suggestions for using specific dialogic tools to overcome specific kinds of problems.

## SIDE CONVERSATIONS: NELSON'S CHALLENGE

### "I Thought at Times I Lost Control of the Conversation"

Nelson Rothfuss and his 12th-grade AP students were just beginning a new unit exploring visual literacies, which included analysis of historical images, paintings, and multimedia texts. Prior to the example lesson that follows, Nelson introduced the idea of reading images. At the end of the unit, students wrote an essay analyzing a single image or a comparison of images. In this example, Nelson led a discussion in which the whole group collaborated to analyze a photograph projected on a screen.

Although the discussion had been generally productive, Nelson felt frustrated by side conversations: "While I like being able to hold conversations this way, I thought at times I lost control of the conversation." He was concerned that when students were chatting among themselves, they not only distracted themselves and therefore missed out on learning from others' ideas in the whole group; they also distracted others. Nelson was also concerned that because he could not "pick up on everything students were saying," he was unable to monitor how students were participating or to assess students' understanding of the text. Finally, Nelson noted that a few students tended to dominate the discussion:

> It seemed that a lot of times the students who led the conversation were simply the ones who were the quickest to respond and the most assertive in their responses. I noticed several times that multiple students would start responding to a question, and the ones who were most assertive were the ones who ended up having their opinions/thoughts heard (the less assertive students simply stopped talking to let the other students speak).

Nelson seemed concerned that many students had attempted to chime in with something to say but had been squeezed out of the conversation by more assertive students. Because he acknowledged that participating in dialogic interactions is important to learning, he wanted to think about how to make space for more student voices.

## MANAGING SIDE CONVERSATIONS

Side conversations and a few dominant students constitute enduring challenges of managing discussions. What can Nelson do to manage these challenges? For starters, it might be worth reconsidering whether a whole-class interaction is the best strategy for meeting the goals of this particular lesson. Many teachers assume that dialogic talk equals whole-group discussion. But that is not necessarily the case. Many possible configurations generate—and help manage—student talk. For example, perhaps small-group conversations would achieve just as much while avoiding the challenges that Nelson encountered. For those who, like Nelson, are working to manage the challenges of side conversations and a few dominant students, we recommend two dialogic tools.

### Think-Pair Share

Rather than asking students to share their "rough draft" talk with the whole group (Smagorinsky, 2008), Nelson could ask each student to turn to the person next to him or her to process thinking in pairs. In the transcript, Nelson asked, "What does this image show about people in the picture?" He could have proceeded to say,

### Inside the Classroom: Nelson's Transcript

**Teacher:** So what does this image show about the people in the picture?
**Tara:** The one doesn't look like she belongs.
**Teacher:** Which one?
**Rebecca:** The one in the middle!
**Walter:** It looks like she does not belong in there. It's creepy.
**Tara:** She's the orphan, she's . . .
**Walter:** That is creepy.
**Teacher:** This one, what makes you think that? What specific things?
[Lots of talking from many.]
**Cecelia:** Her color.
**Tara:** Her clothes.
**Cecelia:** Her clothing is darker and then her skin is . . .
**Tara:** Her posture.
**Walter:** Her hands.
**Anita:** She looks like she wasn't in the picture, like . . .
[Constant inaudible speaking from Cecelia.]
**Walter:** She got Photoshopped in!
**Graham:** She's like . . . she like real pale compared to everyone else.
**Gordon:** She stands out more than everyone else.
[Constant low-volume background conversations.]
**Anita:** Like she's not part of the family or they stick the family in the back and she's not part of it.
**Graham:** Like she just walked on their porch and they're like, "Whatchu doin?"
[Constant inaudible speaking from Cecelia.]
**Teacher:** Why do you say it's a family?
[Lots of talking from many.]

"Please turn to a partner and share a few things you notice." This reconfiguration could serve to (1) harness the energy of the side conversations—taking advantage of the side conversations already happening rather than trying to overcome them; (2) give all students, not just a few assertive students, equal opportunity to talk; and as an added bonus, (3) eliminate the large-group audience for students like Cecelia, who may be feeling tempted to perform. The Think-Pair-Share could function on its own, or it could be followed by a few students sharing their ideas with the large group. Of course every pedagogical decision has both affordances and limitations. It is true that the Think-Pair-Share will mean that Nelson still won't be able to "pick up on everything students say." But Nelson would have to weigh the pros and cons against his goals for student talk.

### A Closer Look: Challenges Related to Student Participation

Many different kinds of challenges can arise when teachers are facilitating dialogic interactions. It is often helpful to begin by identifying what, exactly, the problem is. Here are a few of the enduring challenges we have experienced ourselves and that we have seen in countless classrooms:

- Many students talk at once
- Students have side conversations
- A few students dominate the discussion
- Only a few students participate
- The same few students participate in every session
- Either boys or girls dominate
- Those who talk don't necessarily have the best ideas
- Students who don't participate aren't actively listening either

## Composing Prompt

A composing prompt would be another alternative to consider. In his reflection, Nelson thought he might revise this lesson by asking students to respond to his initial question in writing, which would give students time to think about and develop their answers before sharing them with the large group. Nelson could opt to call on students to share what they wrote rather than waiting for dominant students to volunteer. We also noticed that students responded with quick one- or two-word answers. A composing prompt might help students develop thoughts in more depth, thereby freeing Nelson from having to facilitate so many short turns. Finally, the composing prompt might also offer a few quiet moments to interrupt the boisterous energy. The composing prompt might offer just the right amount of structure to focus students' thoughts and help to harness students' energy.

## QUALITY OF STUDENT RESPONSES: BARBARA'S CHALLENGE

### "I Was a Bit Disappointed . . . No One Takes It to This Deeper Analytical Level"

Over the course of the semester, Barbara McGee had been working on releasing more and more control of discussions to her 12th-grade students (as outlined in Chapter 4). She had worked explicitly with her students to release responsibility to

### Inside the Classroom: Barbara's Transcript

**Ana:** Why would you need so many traps, though?

**Jude:** Cuz it's protecting the inner party—that's the most important part of the party. They're the upper class, they only think of themselves.

**Rob:** They're so afraid of, like, the lower classes rising up that they . . .

**Jude:** That they set up so many traps that they'll know they'll be safe.

**Erin:** The only way for them to have power is to see into everyone's mind.

**Bobbi:** Isn't the proles [working class, proletariat] part of the lower class? So to stop the lower class from rising up, they use the lower class to trap the middle class?

**All:** And the lower class.

**Rob:** Cuz like, they think, this is what I got, they felt like the lower class, they saw them as animals basically, so they, they basically felt like they weren't . . . rise again . . . they thought the real threat was the middle class.

**Jude:** Using the lower class to . . .

**Caleb:** You see, this still bothers me, though, with the telescreen behind the picture frame. Does that mean the guy that was friends with them was part in, with it?

**All:** Ya, he was Thought Police.

**Caleb:** Oh that *is* the guy?

**All:** Yeah.

**Caleb:** Okay. That makes so much more sense then. So, how would you not check behind everything?

---

them for independent discussions. In this particular example, students were engaged in a Socratic seminar, which constituted the summative assessment of the unit on *1984*, by George Orwell. The Socratic seminar was conducted in lieu of a test.

On the one hand, Barbara was pleased that students were able to sustain the discussion without any facilitation or intervention on her part. Their independence in that regard reflected significant growth over the course of the semester. However, Barbara expressed being both excited at their progress and frustrated with the shallowness of the discussion:

> I was a bit disappointed with the amount of comprehension clarification. I realize that students need to clear things up, and also that to discuss plot is inevitable. They mention so many things that could be discussed in greater detail, less with plot and more with individual interpretation. No one takes it to this deeper analytical level than perhaps they could have handled.

### A Closer Look: Challenges Related to the Quality of Student Talk

Once you become more proficient at soliciting and managing participation, you may encounter new challenges in terms of the quality of learning talk. For example, English teachers with whom we have worked have described the following challenges:

- Student talk tends to remain on surface level
- Students share lots of personal stories but don't make connections between their stories and the text
- Students respond in one-word answers or short phrases
- Students talk only to the teacher and not to each other
- Students respond without listening to each other/responding to what others say
- Students' responses are sarcastic, goofy, or not serious

Barbara felt that students' talk seemed to stay on the "surface." What she really desired was for her students to go beyond plot clarification to delve more deeply into analysis, to reach higher levels of critical thinking.

## RAISING THE QUALITY OF STUDENT TALK

Barbara certainly isn't alone in her concern over surface-level talk. What can Barbara do to help students reach toward higher levels of critical thinking during discussion? In this case, we suggest reconsidering the level of teacher involvement. Sometimes teachers interpret the call for more student voices as a call for no teacher voices. In other words, teachers sometimes view the absence of the teacher voice as the gold standard for dialogic interaction. While it is true that student-facilitated dialogic tools, such as Socratic seminars, fishbowls, and literature circles, can be valuable resources, it is also true that achieving high-quality student-led discussions takes a lot of time, instruction, and support. If Barbara's students are not reaching the desired depth of thought on their own, Barbara might consider reintroducing herself as a participant in the discussion and spending more time scaffolding students' participation in high-quality discussion before turning over the reins for a student-led interaction. Here are a few specific suggestions.

## Teacher-Generated Questions

The questions Barbara's students were asking remained at the comprehension level. A few well-designed questions could change the course of this discussion to reach higher levels of critical thinking. Perhaps Barbara could design questions to target analysis, synthesis, or evaluation (Bloom, Engelhart, Furst, Hill, & Krathwohl, 1956). She could either pose those questions herself as a participant in the discussion or she could give the questions to students ahead of time on a handout so they could refer to them themselves. In addition to posing questions, Barbara could participate in the Socratic seminar as a guide who steps in from time to time to push or redirect student talk.

## Handout, Graphic Organizer, or Worksheet

If Barbara felt committed to staying out of the discussion, she might alternatively offer students another kind of tool as a scaffold to use during their Socratic seminar. For example, she could offer students a handout with a few examples of the kinds of questions she hoped to hear during the course of the discussion. Giving students teacher-generated questions ahead of time could also serve to model for students what kinds of questions she was looking for.

Or she and the students could develop a graphic organizer designed to make explicit higher-order thinking skills, such as evaluation, synthesis, and application (Bloom et al., 1956). Students could prepare for the Socratic seminar by designing questions or ideas related to each of these levels of critical thinking and use the graphic organizers as a tool to gauge how well they were demonstrating those kinds of thinking during the discussion.

Another option would be offering students an advance worksheet to help them sort out comprehension-level questions. That tool might help set them up for success transcending comprehension talk during the Socratic seminar.

## INACCURATE AND OFFENSIVE COMMENTS: RAE'S CHALLENGE

### "Most Prisons Are Made Up of a Majority of African American Inmates"

If you initiate a discussion about a complex or controversial topic, you may find that students respond in ways that you did not expect. When veteran teacher Rae and her AP 10th-graders read Lorraine Hansberry's *A Raisin in the Sun*, Rae wanted to discuss racism. Prior to the discussion, Rae presented a PowerPoint slide show with examples of racism today. In response to these examples, she wanted her students to discuss not only historical examples of racism but also the ways racism continues to operate in their own community. Her goals for the unit were

## Inside the Classroom: Rae's Transcript

**Teacher:** You probably already know and have heard through our discussions—it's kind of common knowledge—that most prisons are made up of a majority of African American inmates yet they are a minority in our country. So, you need to think about why that is. Do they either commit more crimes or they're prosecuted more? What do you think is the reason behind this?

**Matt:** I think they commit more crimes just because of where they grew up they probably needed to do more crimes. They can't afford the stuff they need or they are just angry at things so they take it out, um, in bad ways.

**Teacher:** Okay.

**James:** Um, I've heard this before—that they'll commit crimes because they'll get, um, a bed in prison and they can't get it at home.

**Teacher:** It's interesting when the economy first took its hit, there were people that were, you know, they were a majority of African Americans at that point—they were committing crimes and the crime rate does go up and that could be a factor. Sometimes it's safer and healthier in prison, but I'd think that'd be a real slight percent.

**Andrew:** I've heard that too though. Black people will commit crimes just so they could go to jail.

**Sam:** I think it might be cops who are racist toward African Americans so they're more likely to pull over someone who is African American versus White.

**Teacher:** Okay, and I'm sure we could find statistics about African Americans getting harsher sentences than White offenders. Whatever it is, do you think that someone with black skin is just more violent?

**Matt:** Probably.

**Students:** *No!* [Laughing.] Probably not.

**Teacher:** The correct response would be no. So then you would look to sociological issues as to why this happens.

## A Closer Look: Challenges Related to Complex Topics and Controversial Issues

Complex and controversial issues may raise difficult challenges:

- Students may say things that are inaccurate
- They may say things that offend others
- They may say things that transgress against classroom policies of respect and tolerance
- They may disagree with one another
- They may get emotional

Students aren't alone in facing challenges. Teachers also express their own challenges:

- Glossing over complex issues
- Being uninformed on the issue
- Being ill prepared to correct inaccuracies
- Feeling anxious about confronting students' ignorance in front of other students
- Feeling unsure whether "this is English" (i.e., disciplinary talk appropriate for English)

motivated by her view that her students, who lived in a predominantly White community and attended a predominantly White school, were naive about the realities of racism in society today. Specifically, she raised the issue of justice in the legal system by sharing a graph depicting disparate incarceration rates for White men and African American men. As you can see in the transcript that follows, students responded with statements that were inaccurate and reinforced racism through negative stereotypes and misconceptions.

Rae's challenge was not just that students made inaccurate and offensive statements but also that she was not sure how to respond. First, she acknowledged that she did not understand the concept of institutional racism in enough depth to speak extemporaneously to correct students' misconceptions. Second, she felt conflicted about calling attention to an individual student's racist comments in front of the whole class. She feared that by doing so she might shut that student down and discourage other individuals from speaking up on similar topics in the future.

## RESPONDING TO INACCURATE OR
## OFFENSIVE STATEMENTS

Dialogic tools like anticipation guides, take a stand, and Four Corners (Table 3.1) are designed to raise controversial issues that are likely to evoke strong opinions and generate student talk. While these tools can certainly work as a springboard for motivating participation, avoid sending the message of "talk at all costs." As Rae's example illustrates, sometimes talk risks doing more harm than good. So what can you do when students say things that are inaccurate or offensive?

First, consider the purposes of your lesson. English teachers are often encouraged *not* to shy away from difficult issues, such as racism. English education scholars and teacher educators reassure English teachers that they do not have to know all of the answers; they can explore issues along with their students. Addressing these issues imperfectly, the reasoning goes, beats not addressing them at all because ignoring these topics sends students the message that it is not okay to talk about them. While it is important to tackle issues like racism, Rae's example also illustrates that discussions can have unintended consequences. You can mitigate these consequences by articulating clear goals for initiating such talk and preparing yourself to respond to challenges as they arise. We have a few suggestions for making these discussions safe and productive.

### Direct Instruction

Rae's challenge grew out of relying on students' opinions to address a complex topic about which they knew little. Rae assumed that the racism of the American legal system is common knowledge. Although students may be aware that the legal system is unjust, the concept of institutional racism is complex. Many adults, including Rae, have trouble articulating how injustice in the legal system works. Rae might have opted to begin this lesson with direct instruction on the topic of institutional racism. She might have given a lecture based on facts and credible information on the topic of institutional racism. If Rae felt unprepared to provide that instruction herself, she might have invited an expert on the topic to do a guest lecture. This suggestion may seem contrary to the idea that dialogic instruction involves less teacher talk and encourages students not to think of the teacher as the expert on all topics. However, our conception of dialogic tools is based on using the right tool for the right purpose at the right time. We are not suggesting that student-led or student-centered discussions are the only tool in the box. Rather, the teacher has an important role to play. And, at times, direct instruction is the best tool for the job. Sometimes teachers need to introduce students to new ideas and information so they can engage in generative discussion later in the lesson.

## Informational Text

Rae might also consider beginning this lesson with reading an informational text that explains the concept of institutional racism today. It might be an excerpt from a sociology book, a newspaper article or editorial about a contemporary issue, or a narrative about a personal experience with racism. An informational text could offer Rae's students—who admittedly have scant frames of reference for talking about racism—something to discuss, as well as examples on which they could draw.

## Framing Language

Research has also shown that how teachers frame discussions on racism matters enormously (Anagnostopoulos, 2011). In this case, Rae might frame the discussion differently. Rather than asking, "Why do you think that is?", Rae could ask, "How does racism operate in the U.S. legal system?" Rae's initial question frames the issue as a matter of student opinion. The alternative question frames the issue as a concept to be understood. The alternative might help to avoid students' misconceptions.

## Time

Teachers tend to gloss over topics like racism (Haviland, 2008), perhaps because they feel uncomfortable. But surface-level treatment of complex topics can do harm. Although Rae acknowledged deeper, more complex sociological forces accounting for racism in the American legal system, she did not explain to students what those forces are. Rae later explained that they really did not have time to go into it. Time plays a key role in adequately addressing critical issues like racism. Planning on spending an adequate amount of time on discussions about complex issues can help to ensure that students do not walk away from discussions with misconceptions.

## MAKING RECITATION MORE DIALOGIC: KEITH'S CHALLENGE

### "I Was Thrown Off by Todd Responding . . . [in a Way] I Had Not Anticipated"

In Keith Kauffman's English class, the Thursday vocabulary review was part of a weekly vocabulary routine. On Monday, students received a vocabulary list, on Thursday they reviewed for a quiz, and on Friday they took the quiz. Each week, they revisited their goal to learn vocabulary in order to "know and describe their world," as Keith put it. In the following example, Keith and his

## Inside the Classroom: Keith's Transcript

**Teacher:** Why do we study vocab?

**Multiple students:** To know and describe our world.

**Teacher:** To know and describe our world, that's right. Now [changes slide to springtime forest scene], we have a scene here, a beautiful scene. What three vocab words, there's gonna be at least three, think on your vocab words . . . what three vocab words can we use to know and describe our scene here?

**Todd:** *Blithe.* [Pronounces incorrectly.]

**Danielle:** *Blithe.* [Pronounces correctly.]

**Teacher:** Why *blithe?*

**Todd:** It looks joyous and happy.

**Teacher:** Okay, we'll pass on *blithe* there, Todd, even though you can make a case for this scene being joyous and happy. It's good that you know that word, though. Tavia?

**Tavia:** This scene looks sylvan.

**Teacher:** Sylvan. You say *sylvan.* Why *sylvan?*

**Tavia:** Because *sylvan* means trees, and we see that the scene shows a woods.

**Teacher:** Pertaining to trees, right. *Sylvan* is the first word we see that can describe this scene. Write down the word *sylvan,* so you can practice writing it down, spelling it correctly. Katrina?

**Katrina:** Couldn't you say this scene is unpremeditated?

**Teacher:** Unpremeditated . . . .why do you say that?

**Katrina:** Because the woods grow spontaneously; it does it in an unpremeditated manner.

**Teacher:** Wow. Guys, let's listen. Katrina said *unpremeditated* . . . and why?

**Katrina:** Because the woods grow in an unplanned manner.

**Teacher:** I wish I would have thought of that . . . I could have made this four vocab words. Unpremeditated . . . good. Amelia, were you going to say *unpremeditated?*

students are in the 16th week of vocabulary study. For this lesson, Keith creat-ed a PowerPoint slide show with pictures to spark students' exchange of ideas about using words from the week's list. In the transcript excerpt, students are volunteering answers to the question of which vocabulary words best describe a wooded scene.

Although the lesson went smoothly enough, Keith, who was working delib-erately on going dialogic, expressed frustration with how it went. In particular, he felt he had been inconsistent in how he responded to students' answers. He explained:

> I was thrown off by Todd responding with a word that I had not anticipated being part of the scene. I initially praised him for a good effort at logical support. However, my next move was to move on and look for words that "better fit" the setting. [A few moments later], I responded with praise to Katrina who . . . also presented a word . . . that . . . was not outlined as a possibility in my lesson plan.

While Keith saw some validity in Todd's response, he opted to guide Todd toward one of the words Keith had in mind. But when Katrina responded in a similar way, Keith accepted Katrina's response even thought it was not the response he was looking for. Keith was not certain whether, why, or when to accept some students' answers and not others'.

Although Keith did not articulate the challenge this way himself, we see Keith's challenge—manifested as inconsistent responses to students' answers—as the result of an underlying tension between his expressed dialogic goals and his choice to use recitation, an instructional format that does not invite sus-tained learning talk. On the one hand, Keith expressed dialogic goals: His lesson plan framed the purpose of the vocabulary lesson as helping students to bet-ter know and describe their world; he wanted students to discuss their weekly words and build their vocabulary organically; he wanted them to collaborate on generating their own ideas for using specific words. On the other hand, Keith's lesson mobilized the default classroom tool of recitation: He designed a prompt (the slides) with particular answers in mind, thereby positioning himself as the arbiter of right and wrong answers, a move that created tension with his expressed dialogic goals. He proceeded to facilitate talk by doing most of the questioning and evaluating. Moreover, the culmination of the week's work—the Friday quiz—was oriented toward single, right answers. In Keith's lesson plan, moreover, he framed his yearlong vocabulary routine as preparation for the ACT college entrance exam, a high-stakes test based on single, right answers. The conflicting goals at the heart of this vocabulary lesson created challenges for Keith in responding to students' unexpected answers.

## APPROACHING KNOWN-ANSWER CONTENT
## FROM A DIALOGIC STANCE

Keith wants to engage students in a dialogic exploration of vocabulary. He also wants to prepare them for the Friday quiz featuring known-answer questions. Although these two goals do not have to be mutually exclusive, the two different goals seem to be creating a challenge for Keith, a challenge that might be similar to those preparing students for the ACT or other standardized test, or working within the Common Core language standards, while also pursuing dialogic goals. What can Keith and others do to negotiate dialogic teaching with seemingly known-answer content such as vocabulary and test prep? Consider delineating these two goals. We have suggestions for going in either direction and a third suggestion for a middle ground.

### Dialogic Assignments/Assessments

On the one hand, if Keith wants to pursue the goal of students exploring vocabulary to "know and describe their world," he might have more success generating the dialogic interaction he desires by adjusting the original prompt slightly. For example, rather than preparing PowerPoint slides for three vocabulary words in mind ahead of time, Keith might simply ask students to collaborate together to create their own slides to represent particular vocabulary words. Maybe students would share their slides with the large group and explain how the slide represents their word. The main difference between these two prompts is that Keith had had three predetermined answers in mind for his original prompt, while the alternative prompt is more open-ended.

### Dialogic Stance

On the other hand, Keith might go about vocabulary study in a different way. For the quiz and the ACT, the goal is less about selecting our own words to describe our world and more about remembering words and their meanings for recall on the test. Even though test preparation involves memorizing words and definitions, helping students remember words and definitions can be approached in a dialogic way. For example, Keith could invite students to collaborate on making up mnemonic devices for remembering words and definitions. He could ask students to make up skits that incorporate several of the week's vocabulary words and definitions. He could ask students to draw pictures or create other artwork to help them remember words and definitions. Or they might have a discussion about the words.

## Opening Discussion About the Words and Images

Another option could involve leaving much of the lesson in place but pursuing students' unexpected ideas and contributions to build more cumulative talk. Such cumulative talk could actually help the words stick in students' memories for the quiz and for their literate lives beyond the quiz. For example, when Keith does follow Katrina's unexpected response, he says, "Wow. Guys, let's listen. Katrina said unpremeditated . . . and why?" and then, "I wish I would have thought of that . . . I could have made this four vocab words. Unpremeditated . . . good. Amelia, were you going to say unpremeditated?" These responses seem promising, for example Keith's uptake question, "Why?" which required that she explain the meaning of the word in connection with the scene. It is an uptake question and, we think, an authentic question. We also wonder if the humor lacing through the conversation may help students remember the words—we see that too as promising because students seemed highly engaged. But pursuing openings created by students like Katrina sharing their reasoning to elicit further talk about words (i.e., *unpremeditated*) could help deepen students' understanding of and capacity to remember vocab words. It might also pique and sustain curiosity about words and their relationships to other words. For example, Keith might have responded to Katrina's reply with a remark such as "Your comment raises an interesting distinction between *unplanned* and *unpremeditated*. Let's think more about that." In referring back to his own lesson planning, Keith discourages exploratory thinking and talk that could help the words implant themselves indelibly in students' memories.

For Keith, and for all teachers, it can be comforting to remember that leading high-quality learning talk can be challenging for English teachers of all experience levels. Yet it need not always be this way. You need not settle for mediocre learning talk and you need not abandon all hope of dialogue if you face challenges. In fact, if you think about your teaching as a process of drafting, you should *expect* challenges. You can then reassure yourself that students' participation in learning talk can improve with practice, as you respond to the challenges that emerge by calling upon specific tools and strategies for dialogic teaching. The payoff for student learning and achievement is worth the effort.

# Overview of Teachers and Curriculum

| Chapter | Teacher Name | Grade(s) | Subject | Curriculum |
|---------|--------------|----------|---------|------------|
| 1 | Jackie Loper | 10 | American Literature | *The Crucible*, by Arthur Miller |
| 2 | Jackie Loper* | 10 | American Literature | *The Crucible*, by Arthur Miller |
| 3 | Elnora Greenstein | 10 | English Language Arts | *Great Expectations*, by Charles Dickens |
| | Logan Cloe | 9–12 | Media Studies | *Feed*, by M. T. Anderson |
| | Caroline Weekley | 10–11 | American Composition and Literature | *Fahrenheit 451*, by Ray Bradbury |
| | Kimberly Longley* | 12 | English Literature I (British Literature) | *Frankenstein*, by Mary Shelley |
| 4 | Melinda Vallarta | 11 | Honors World Literature | *The Iliad*, by Homer *The Canterbury Tales*, by Chaucer *Hamlet*, by William Shakespeare |
| | Krista Delafuente | 9 | Pre–Advanced Placement English | "Oranges," by Gary Soto |

*(continued)*

## Overview of Teachers and Curriculum *(continued)*

| Chapter | Teacher Name | Grade(s) | Subject | Curriculum |
|---------|-------------|----------|---------|-----------|
| 5 | Libby Ancheta* | 10 | English 10A: American English | Argument (position paper) writing |
| | Lucia Elden*,† | First-year college students and secondary students | Dual-Enrolled College Composition | Argumentative review writing |
| 6 | Madelyn Napier | 11 | British Literature | *Frankenstein,* by Mary Shelley |
| | Krista Delafuente | 9 | Pre–Advanced Placement English | *The Great Gatsby* by F. Scott Fitzgerald |
| 7 | Melissa Sherr | 11–12 | Advanced Placement Composition | Introduction to Toulmin method of writing arguments |
| | Libby Ancheta | 10 | English 10A: American English | Argument (position paper) writing |
| Coda | Nelson Rothfuss | 12 | Advanced Placement Writing and Composition | Visual Literacies unit |
| | Barbara McGee | 12 | English 11 | *1984,* by George Orwell |
| | Rae Belmont | 10 | Pre–Advanced Placement English | *A Raisin in the Sun,* by Lorraine Hansberry |
| | Keith Kauffman | 11 | English | Vocabulary review |

*Indicates reproducible materials included in example.

†Indicates real name: All others are pseudonyms.

# Research Methodology

## Video-Based Response and Reflection: A 2-Year Study of English Teacher Candidates' Development of Dialogic Instructional Practices

Throughout the book we mention findings from our study of new teachers developing dialogic instruction. Now we briefly describe the research methods grounding our arguments. For more detail on the English education curricular and pedagogical design, see Juzwik et al. (2012) and Heintz et al. (2010). For more detail on the research methodology and results, see Caughlan et al. (2013).

### Design of the Study

We designed Video-Based Response and Revision (VBRR) in response to a continuing issue in English teacher education—the difficulty of preparing teacher candidates to engage in dialogic instruction. The study took place within the English teacher preparation program at a major midwestern university's college of education, where teacher candidates take professional education coursework, including practicum experiences; complete BA degrees in content areas; and complete year-long, post-BA internships. All teacher candidates who went through the program during the 2-year period were invited to participate. Because we realized that the relationship between the university classroom and the secondary classroom is complicated, and that any intervention will have unexpected consequences, we chose to make this a design-based study so that we could revise our curriculum and our research study as we learned with our participants (Cobb, Confrey, diSessa, Lehrer, & Schauble, 2003; Reinking & Bradley, 2008).

Five research questions guided our investigation of the outcomes of VBRR:

- Given participation in VBRR, what patterns of tool use characterize teacher candidates' planning for dialogically organized instruction?
- Given participation in VBRR, to what extent do teacher candidates make use of dialogic discourse moves in their teaching?
- To what extent did an increased use of dialogic tools in planning relate to an increase in dialogic questioning?

- To what extent did the use of dialogic tools relate to the level of student participation?
- What is the relationship among patterns of dialogic tool use in planning, teachers' questions, contextual factors, and student participation? In short, what is the relationship between planning for and achievement of dialogic instruction?

*Contexts*. During the internship year, teacher candidates were assigned to a variety of teaching contexts. Most (79%) were in high schools. Thirty-six percent were in urban and 53% in suburban locations, with the remaining few in town or rural schools. Almost half the teacher candidates were placed in schools reflecting a range of racial and economic diversity.

Over the year, teachers progressively assumed more teaching responsibilities until they were "lead teaching" several periods a day. They also completed courses designed to support their work as early career professionals, including a sequence of two English methods courses in which the research took place. VBRR involved teacher candidates in four key activities:

- Becoming aware of different kinds of learning talk and their implications for student learning;
- Planning lessons that aimed for dialogically organized instruction;
- Using videorecordings of their teaching to engage in self and peer response, reflection, and revising their instruction; and
- Engaging in online learning communities where they collaboratively supported each other's developing dialogic teaching practices.

*Participants*. Eighty-seven teacher candidates from two intern cohorts participated in the research over the 2 years (69 were women, 18 men). All but two were traditional students in their early 20s. Both cohorts were predominately White, with two teacher candidates self-identifying as Hispanic, two as African American, and one as multiracial. All four book authors collaborated on methods course curriculum design and all taught sections of the courses in which VBRR was enacted.

*Data*. Data analyzed for this study included video posts completed by teacher candidates in focal English methods courses. Each video post included (1) a 5-minute video clip, (2) contextualizing material (including lesson plan), (3) a transcript of the video clip, (4) responses to the video clip by fellow group members, and (5) a written reflection on the process.

First, teacher candidates videotaped themselves teaching an entire class period and selected one 5-minute clip of whole-class interaction to share with a small group of colleagues. Second, candidates prepared contextualizing materials, including their plan for the lesson, descriptions of their teaching contexts and courses, the curricular goals relevant to the lesson highlighted in the video clip, and specific challenges with classroom management or instruction. In their contextualizing materials, candidates also posed questions to their colleagues to focus feedback on particular areas of need. Third, teacher candidates transcribed their 5-minute clips and posted video clips, contextualizing materials, and transcripts on a secure, online social networking site. Fourth, colleagues in small online groups viewed each other's videos and provided feedback and responses. Finally, using writing, audio, or video, teacher candidates composed a reflection on the process, responding to colleagues' feedback with an eye toward generating revisions, refinements, and ideas for future teaching.

Each video post assignment built on the one before, encouraging teacher candidates to critically engage with some specific aspect of dialogic instruction (see Juzwik et al., 2012 for more detail on video post design). Teacher candidates in Cohort 1 completed the video post process four times, and those in Cohort 2 completed the process three times. For this study, we analyzed all text documents associated with video posts completed by participating teacher candidates in over 300 lessons.

*Measures.* To answer our research questions, we coded for four main types of variables: (1) basic contextual information, (2) the number and kind of dialogic tools used in planning, (3) the nature of teacher instructional discourse, and (4) the extent of student participation in classroom discourse. (See vbrr.wiki.educ. msu.edu/Analytic+tools to see the coding manual we developed, with our complete list of coding categories.)

To characterize teacher candidates' planning for dialogically organized instruction (Research Question 1), we coded the planning documents posted with the videos for dialogic tools and further categorized tools according to whether they were teacher led or student led. Because categories and distinct types of dialogic tools coded in the study emerged from inductive analysis of a particular collection of lesson plans and contextualizing materials, the list does not include all possible dialogic tools teachers might use.

Given our interest in teacher candidates' achievement of dialogic instruction in practice (Research Question 2), we used indicators of the nature of teacher discourse (dialogic vs. monologic), including teacher authentic questions, teacher nonauthentic questions, teacher uptake, and teacher revoicing of student utterances.

Because it allowed us to relate teacher planning and practice to student discourse (Research Questions 4 and 5), we measured the ratio of student participation in classroom discourse to teacher participation to indicate accomplishment of dialogic instruction in the study. We therefore examined the ratio of student to teacher utterances, where utterances were distinguished by a change in speaker (*S2Tratio*). We calculated *S2Tratio* for each lesson as: $\sum$ Student utterances / ($\sum$ Student utterances + $\sum$ Teacher utterances). Where the teacher maintains control over each classroom interaction (i.e., in recitation, where the teacher poses a question and the student responds) we would see an *S2Tratio* of .5. In contrast, a lesson consisting entirely of student-led discussion with no teacher utterances would generate a value of 1.0. Although quantity is not the only important aspect of student participation, this number enabled us to consider teachers' relative success in getting students to participate and respond to each other.

Before coding, researchers and coders devised a coding manual and coded several common files to refine categories. We coded additional common files until we consistently reached agreement on coding categories. The team met regularly during coding to discuss and resolve problematic examples; these discussions maintained a common understanding of coding categories throughout the process.

*Analysis.* Analysis occurred in several stages. To address Research Questions 1 and 2, we calculated descriptive statistics on the extent and variability in teachers' use of dialogic tools and on teachers' use of such dialogic moves as revoicing, uptake, and authentic questions. In response to Research Question 3, we compiled basic inferential statistics (Spearman's rank order correlation coefficients) examining the association between teachers' use of dialogic tools and the nature of teacher questions. Guided by Research Question 4, we dug deeper, investigating the reduced-form relationship between use of dialogic tools and student participation in classroom discourse. Finally, to answer Research Question 5, we used regression models to consider both the direct effect of dialogic tools on student participation in classroom discourse and the extent to which the effect of dialogic tool use may have been influenced by teachers' use of dialogic questions.

Because each teacher submitted three or more lessons to be analyzed, we also looked at the selection bias. If some teachers were just better at engaging in dialogic instruction, their skills might have made it look like the use of dialogic tools was more important than it actually was. To isolate this factor, we used fixed-effects models to isolate the *within-teacher* variance in classroom instruction, because fixed-effects models provide a strong control for this kind of selection bias (Dee & West, 2011; Guo & VanWey, 1999; Kelly & Carbonaro, 2012).

## Summary of Findings

We found pervasive use of dialogic tools in the planning documents submitted by the teacher candidates. They also used a higher percentage of authentic questions and questions with uptake than would be expected from novice teachers. Although we found a significant effect of teachers' authentic questioning and use of uptake on student participation, we discovered a stronger relationship between planning for dialogic instruction using dialogic tools and student participation. This relationship seemed particularly strong when only student-led tools were considered. When we added the possible contributions of school contextual variables and the effects of the individual teacher, we still found dialogic tool use explaining more variance in student participation than any other factor.

Thus, our analysis finds planning for dialogic teaching strongly associated with its achievement as indicated by high levels of dialogic teacher discourse and student participation. As novice teachers used a wide variety of dialogic tools to prepare for and organize dialogic interaction, they disrupted the historically default classroom discourse patterns in secondary English, such as the dominance of teacher test questions and recitation. Our analysis contributes to research on dialogic teaching in English language arts classrooms by pointing to planning, and specifically the use of dialogic tools in planning, as a key focus for dialogic teacher development. Dialogic tools appeared to offer teachers and students physical and cognitive assistance with the profound challenges of promoting student learning talk and disrupting the turn-taking practices usually found in English language arts classrooms.

# References

Adler, M., & Rougle, E. (2005) *Building literacy through classroom discussion: Research-based strategies for developing critical readers and thoughtful writers in middle school.* New York: Scholastic.

Alexander, R. (2001). *Culture and pedagogy: International comparisons in primary education.* Oxford, UK: Blackwell.

Alexander, R. (2008). *Towards Dialogic Teaching: Rethinking classroom talk* (4th ed.). North Yorkshire, UK: Dialogos.

Anagnostopoulos, D. (2011). *Teaching* To Kill a Mockingbird *in 21st century American classrooms: Sparking and sustaining discussions of race and racism in the English classroom.* Unpublished manuscript, College of Education, Michigan State University, East Lansing, MI.

Angelo, T. A., & Cross, K. P. (1993). *Classroom assessment techniques* (2nd ed.). San Francisco: Jossey-Bass.

Applebee, A. N. (1996). *Curriculum as conversation: Transforming traditions of teaching and learning.* Chicago: University of Chicago Press.

Applebee, A. N., Langer, J. A., Nystrand, M., & Gamoran, A. (2003). Discussion-based approaches to developing understanding: Classroom instruction and student performance in middle and high school English. *American Educational Research Journal, 40*(3), 685–730.

Aristotle. (1991). *On rhetoric: A theory of civic discourse.* (G. Kennedy, Trans.). New York: Oxford University Press.

Bakhtin, M. M. (1981). *The dialogic imagination.* (M. Holquist, Ed.; C. Emerson & M. Holquist, Trans.). Austin: University of Texas Press. (Original work published 1935)

Barnes, D. (1976). *Communication and the curriculum.* London: Penguin.

Beach, R., & Myers, J. (2001) *Inquiry-based English instruction: Engaging students in life and literature.* New York: Teachers College Press.

Bloom, B. S., Engelhart, M. D., Furst, E. J., Hill, W. H., & Krathwohl, D. R. (1956). *Taxonomy of educational objectives: The classification of educational goals; Handbook I: Cognitive Domain.* New York: Longmans, Green.

Boyd, M., & Galda, L. (2011). *Real talk in elementary classrooms: Effective oral language practice.* New York: Guilford.

Boyd, M., & Markarian, P. (2011). Dialogic teaching: Talk in service of a dialogic stance. *Language and Education, 25*(6), 515–534.

Britton, J. (1989). *Language, the learner, and the school.* Portsmouth, NH: Heinemann. (Original work published 1969)

Burke, J. (2010). *What's the big idea? Question-driven units to motivate reading, writing, and thinking.* Portsmouth, NH: Heinemann.

Burke, K. (1972). *The philosophy of literary form.* New York: Vintage. (Original work published 1941)

Caughlan, S. (2011, April). *The standards movement vs. the pastoral tradition in literature teaching: Fewer, clearer, and higher?* Paper presented at the Fourth Guy Bond Memorial Conference, St. Paul, Minnesota.

Caughlan, S., Juzwik, M. M., Borsheim-Black, C., Kelly, S., & Fine, J. (2013). English teacher candidates developing dialogically organized instructional practices. *Research in the Teaching of English, 47*(3), 212–246.

Caughlan, S., & Kelly, S. (2004). Bridging methodological gaps: Instructional and institutional effects of tracking in two English classes. *Research in the Teaching of English, 39,* 20–62.

Christenbury, L., & Kelly, P. P. (1983). *Questioning: A path to critical thinking.* Urbana, IL: National Council of Teachers of English.

Christoph, J. N., & Nystrand, M. (2002). Taking risks, negotiating relationships: One teacher's transition toward a dialogic classroom. *Research in the Teaching of English, 36,* 249–281.

Cobb, P., Confrey, J., diSessa, A., Lehrer, R., & Schauble, L. (2003). Design experiments in educational research. *Educational Researcher, 32*(1), 9–13.

Collins, J. (1982). Discourse style, classroom interaction, and differential treatment. *Journal of Reading Behavior, 14,* 429–437.

Common Core State Standards Initiative (CCSS Initiative). (2010). *Common Core State Standards for English language arts and literacy.* Washington, DC: Council of Chief State School Officers & National Governor's Association. Retrieved from www.core-standards.org/assets/CCSSI_ELA%20Standards.pdf

Conference on College Composition and Communication. (1974). *Students' right to their own language.* Urbana, IL: National Council of Teachers of English.

Connolly, W., & Smith, M. W. (2002). Teachers and students talk about talk: Class discussions and the way it should be. *Journal of Adolescent and Adult Literacy, 46,* 16–26.

Cushman, E. (2012). *The Cherokee syllabary: Writing the people's perseverance.* Norman: University of Oklahoma Press.

Dawson, C. (2011, June). *Revising teaching practices: Framing teaching practices as "texts" in writing workshops.* Paper presented at the Conference on English Education. New York.

Dee, T., & West, M. (2011). The non-cognitive returns to class size. *Educational Evaluation and Policy Analysis, 33,* 23–36.

Department for Education. (2011). Teaching and learning resources. Retrieved from webarchive.nationalarchives.gov.uk/20110809091832/http:/teachingandlearningresources.org.uk/secondary/english

Dewey, J. (2012). *Democracy and education: An introduction to the philosophy of education.* New York: Simon & Brown. (Original work published 1916)

Duffy, J. M. (2011). *Writing from these roots: Literacy in a Hmong-American community.* Manoa: University of Hawaii Press.

Duke, N. K., Caughlan, S., Juzwik, M. M., & Martin, N. M. (2012). *Reading and writing genre with purpose in K–8 classrooms.* Portsmouth, NH: Heinemann.

Falk, J. K., & Drayton, B. (2009). *Creating and sustaining online professional learning communities.* New York: Teachers College Press.

Freire, P. (1970). *Pedagogy of the oppressed.* New York: Seabury.

Gee, J. P. (2008). *Social linguistics and literacies: Ideology in discourses* (3rd ed.). London: Routledge.

Glasser, H., & Easley, J. (2008). *Transforming the difficult child: The nurtured heart approach.* Tucson, AZ: Howard Glasser & Jennifer Easley.

Graff, G., & Birkenstein, K. (2009). *They say/I say: The moves that matter in academic writing.* New York: Norton.

Guo, G., & VanWey, L. K. (1999). Sibship size and intellectual development: Is the relationship causal? *American Sociological Review, 64,* 169–187.

Harris, D. (1996). Assessing discussion of public issues: A scoring guide. In R. W. Evans & D. W. Saxe (Eds.), *Handbook on teaching social issues* (pp. 288–297). Washington, DC: National Council for the Social Studies.

Hatch, T., & Pointer-Mace, D. (2007). Making teaching public: A digital exhibition. *Teachers College Record.* Retrieved from www.tcrecord.org/makingteachingpublic/

Haviland, V. (2008). Things get glossed over: Rearticulating the silencing power of whiteness in education. *Journal of Teacher Education, 59*(1), 40–54.

Heintz, A., Borsheim, C., Caughlan, S., Juzwik, M. M., & Sherry, M. B. (2010). Video-based response and revision: Dialogic instruction using video and Web 2.0 technologies. *Contemporary Issues in Technology and Teacher Education, 10*(2). Retrieved from www.citejournal.org/vol10/iss2/languagearts/article2.cfm

Hess, D. (2009). *Controversy in the classroom: The democratic power of discussion.* New York: Routledge.

Hess, D., & Posselt, J. (2002). High school discussion of controversial public issues. *Journal of Curriculum and Supervision 17,* 285–314.

Hillocks, G. (2011). *Teaching argument writing, grades 6–12: Supporting claims with relevant evidence and clear reasoning.* Portsmouth, NH: Heinemann.

Jenkins, H. (2006). *Convergence culture: Where old and new media collide.* New York: New York University Press.

Johnson, T. S., Thompson, L., Smagorinsky, P., & Fry, P. G. (2003). Learning to teach the five-paragraph theme. *Research in the Teaching of English, 38,* 136–176.

Johnston, P. H. (2012). *Opening minds: Using language to change lives.* Portland, ME: Stenhouse.

Juzwik, M. M. (2010). Negotiating moral stance in classroom discussion about literature: Entextualization and contextualization processes in a narrative spell. In P. Prior & J. Hengst (Eds.), *Exploring semiotic remediation as discourse practice* (pp. 77–106). London: Palgrave Macmillan.

Juzwik, M. M. (2013). Extending the conversation: The ethics of teaching disturbing pasts: Reader response, historical contextualization, and rhetorical (con)textualization of Holocaust texts in English. *English Education, 45*(3), 284–308.

Juzwik, M. M., Anagnotopoulos, D., Whyte, K., Ferkany, M., & Calabrese-Barton, A. (2011). *The pedagogy of dialogue and deliberation across disciplines.* Unfunded grant proposal. East Lansing: Michigan State University.

Juzwik, M. M., Sherry, M., Caughlan, S., Heintz, A., & Borsheim-Black, C. (2012). Supporting dialogically organized instruction in an English teacher preparation program: A video-based, Web 2.0–mediated response and revision pedagogy. *Teachers College Record, 114*(3), 1–42.

Kelly, S. (2007). Classroom discourse and the distribution of student engagement. *Social Psychology of Education, 10,* 331–352.

Kelly, S. (2008). Race, social class, and student engagement in middle school English classrooms. *Social Science Research,* 37, 434–448.

Kelly, S.. & Carbonaro, W. (2012). Curriculum tracking and teacher expectations: Evidence from discrepant course taking models. *Social Psychology of Education, 15,* 271–294.

Kong, A., & Pearson, P. D. (2003). The road to participation: The construction of a literacy practice in a learning community of linguistically diverse learners. *Research in the Teaching of English, 38*(1), 85–124.

Kunzman, R. (2006). *Grappling with the good: Talking about religion and morality in public schools.* Albany: State University of New York Press.

Langer, J. A. (1995) *Envisioning literature: Literary understanding and literature instruction.* New York: Teachers College Press.

Langer, J. A. (2001). Beating the odds: Teaching middle and high school students to read and write well. *American Educational Research Journal, 38*(4), 837–880.

Langer, J. A. (2010). *Envisioning knowledge: Building literacy in the academic disciplines.* New York: Teachers College Press.

Luhrman, B. (Producer & Director). (1996). *Romeo and Juliet* [Motion picture]. USA: Twentieth Century Fox.

Luke, A., Woods, A., & Weir, K. (Eds). (2013). *Curriculum, syllabus design, and equity: A primer and model.* New York: Routledge.

Matanzo, J. B. (1996). Discussion: Assessing what was said and what was done. In L. Gambrell & J. Almasi (Eds.), *Lively discussions! Fostering engaged reading* (pp. 250–264). Newark, DE: International Reading Association.

Matusov, E. (2009). *Journey into dialogic pedagogy.* New York: Nova.

Mehan, H. (1979). *Learning lessons.* Cambridge, MA: Harvard University Press.

Mercer, N. (2000). *Words and minds: How we use language to think together.* London: Routledge.

Moje, E. B. (2007). Developing socially-just subject matter instruction: A review of the literature on disciplinary literacy teaching. *Review of Research in Education 31,* 1–44.

Moore, D. (2007). *Overcoming religious illiteracy.* London: Palgrave Macmillan.

Murphy, P. K., Wilkinson, I. A. G., Soter, A. O., Hennessy, M. N., & Alexander, J. F. (2009). Examining the effects of classroom discussion on students' comprehension of text: A meta-analysis. *Journal of Educational Psychology, 101*(3), 740–764.

Nystrand, M. (with Gamoran, A., Kachur, R., & Prendergast, C.) (1997). *Opening dialogue: Understanding the dynamics of language and learning in the English classroom.* New York: Teachers College Press.

Nystrand, M., & Graff, N. (2001). Report in argument's clothing: An ecological perspective on writing instruction. *The Elementary School Journal, 101,* 470–493.

Nystrand, M., Wu, L. L., Gamoran, A., Zeiser, S., & Long, D. (2003). Questions in time: Investigating the structure and dynamics of unfolding classroom discourse. *Discourse Processes, 35,* 135–198.

O'Donnell-Allen, C. (2011). *Tough talk, tough texts: Teaching English to change the world.* Portsmouth, NH: Heinemann.

Office for Standards in Education, Children's Services and Skills. (2011). *Excellence in English: What we can learn from twelve outstanding schools.* Manchester, UK: Authors. Retrieved from www.ofsted.gov.uk/resources/excellence-english

Purcell-Gates, V. (1997). *Other people's words: The cycle of low literacy.* Cambridge, MA: Harvard University Press.

Raphael, T., Highfield, K., & Au, K. H. (2006). *QAR now: A powerful and practical framework that develops comprehension and higher-order thinking in all students.* New York: Scholastic.

Reinking, D., & Bradley, B. A. (2008). *Formative and design experiments: Approaches to language and literacy research.* New York: Teachers College Press.

Rex, L. A., & Schiller, L. (2009). *Using discourse analysis to improve classroom interaction.* New York: Routledge.

Reznitskaya, A., Anderson, R. C., & McNurlen, B. (2001). Influence of oral discussion on written argument. *Discourse Processes, 32*(2 & 3), 155–175.

Rymes, B. (2009). *Classroom discourse analysis: A tool for critical reflection.* New York: Hampton Press.

Sarroub, L. (2005). *All-American Yemeni girls: Being Muslim in a public school.* Philadelphia: University of Pennsylvania Press.

Sisk-Hilton, S. (2009). *Teaching and learning in public: Professional development through shared inquiry.* New York: Teachers College Press.

Smagorinsky, P. (2002). *Teaching English through principled practice.* Upper Saddle River, NJ: Merill/Prentice Hall.

Smagorinsky, P. (2008). *Teaching English by design: How to create and carry out instructional units.* Portsmouth, NH: Heinemann.

Smitherman, G. (1977). *Talkin and testifyin: The language of Black America.* Detroit: Wayne State University Press.

Thompson, P. (2008). Learning through extended talk. *Language and Education, 22*(3), 241–256.

Toulmin, S. (1958). *The uses of argument.* Cambridge: University of Cambridge Press.

Vinz, R. (1996). *Composing a teaching life.* Portsmouth, NH: Boynton Cook.

Wilhelm, J. (2007). *Engaging readers and writers with inquiry: Promoting deep understandings in language arts and the content areas with guiding questions.* New York: Scholastic.

# Index

# About the Authors

*Mary M. Juzwik* is associate professor of language and literacy in the Department of Teacher Education (TE) at Michigan State University (MSU). She teaches undergraduate and graduate courses in writing, discourse, and English education. She is an affiliate of the Rhetoric, Writing, and American Cultures Program and the English department at MSU and a principal investigator at the Literacy Achievement Research Center. Mary holds degrees in English from the University of Wisconsin, Madison (PhD), Middlebury College (MA), and Wheaton College (BA). She studies issues related to literacy teaching and learning, including dialogic teaching and teacher preparation; the moral and rhetorical dimensions of teaching; linguistic, cultural, and religious diversity in English classrooms; writing theory and instruction; and teacher identity. Mary's interdisciplinary work on these issues engages with scholarly traditions such as narrative studies, interactional sociolinguistics, and rhetorical theory. Mary received the Edward B. Fry Book Award from the Literacy Research Association for her book *The Rhetoric of Teaching: Understanding the Dynamics of Holocaust Narratives in an English Classroom* (2009). She coedited *Narrative Discourse Analysis for Teacher Educators: Managing Cultural Differences in Classrooms* (2011), coauthored *Reading and Writing Genre with Purpose in K–8 Classrooms* (2012), and has published numerous articles, essays, reviews, and commentaries. She coedits the journal *Research in the Teaching of English*. Learn more about her work at juzwik.wiki.educ.msu.edu/.

*Carlin Borsheim-Black* is assistant professor of English language and literature at Central Michigan University (CMU), where she teaches English methods and young adult literature courses. Her scholarship and service are focused on reinventing literature curriculum and instruction for critical English education, navigating the challenges of doing multicultural work in predominantly White teaching contexts, and continually improving English teacher education. Before joining the faculty at CMU, Carlin earned master's and doctorate degrees at Michigan State University (MSU). During her time at MSU, she was recognized with an Excellence and Innovation in Teaching Award for her work with preservice teachers. Carlin previously taught high school English, drama and creative writing in Michigan and Ohio. She is affiliated with the Red Cedar Writing Project and

Chippewa River Writing Projects. Her work has been published in *English Journal*, *Teachers College Record*, and *Research in the Teaching of English*.

**Samantha Caughlan** is an assistant professor of English education in the Department of Teacher Education at Michigan State University. She taught for 10 years as a high school English and drama teacher in central Wisconsin and currently teaches preservice courses in English methods, as well as master's and doctoral courses on issues related to English education and discourse analysis. She conducts research on English teachers' cultural models as providing insight into their conceptions of their discipline, teaching, and students. She has been long interested in curricular reform, and her recent projects look into the effects of policy on state and local curriculum. She has published articles in *Language Arts*, *Research in the Teaching of English*, *English Education*, *Educational Researcher*, *Yearbook of the National Reading Conference*, and *Educational Policy Analysis Archives*.

**Anne Heintz** is an adjunct professor in the Master of Arts in Educational Technology program at Michigan State University. She was awarded an Excellence and Innovation in Teaching Award from Michigan State University College of Education. Her research interests include studying the use of technologies and the arts for literacy learning in educational and community settings. She coedited the book *Putting Writing Research into Practice: Applications for Teacher Professional Development*. Her work has been published in *Contemporary Issues in Technology and Teacher Education* and *The Journal of Education*. Her website is sites.google.com/site/heintzprofessional/.

"Real talk. Real classrooms. Real students. The authors of *Inspiring Dialogue* have given teacher education programs a tool for introducing dialogic teaching in culturally and linguistically diverse classrooms while meeting Common Core State Standards objectives."

—**Maisha T. Winn**, Susan J. Cellmer Chair in English Education,
University of Wisconsin–Madison, author of *Girl Time: Literacy, Justice, and the School-to-Prison Pipeline*

"*Inspiring Dialogue* covers a comprehensive and practical set of tools and strategies for implementing dialogic instruction.... It is a program that has been fully tested at Michigan State University in one of the most thorough and carefully crafted teacher education programs nationally."

—From the Foreword by **Martin Nystrand**,
Louise Durham Mead Professor of English Emeritus,
professor of education emeritus, University of Wisconsin–Madison

"One of the most exciting aspects of English language arts is the discussion that can occur in the classroom. For many teachers, however, it is often a struggle to structure and implement real dialogue. *Inspiring Dialogue* provides specific guidance to encourage authentic conversations between teachers and students with practical advice for implementation."

—**Leila Christenbury**, chair, Department of Teaching and Learning,
Commonwealth Professor, English Education, School of Education,
Virginia Commonwealth University

*Inspiring Dialogue* helps new English teachers make dialogic teaching practices a central part of ~~~~~~~~~~~~ while also supporting veteran teachers who wo~~~~~~~~~~~~ talk in their classrooms. Chapter by chapter, the book follows novice ~~~~~~ they build a repertoire of practices for planning for, carrying out, and assessing their efforts at dialogic teaching across the secondary English curriculum. The text also covers dialogic teacher learning communities using video study and discourse analysis. Providing a thorough discussion of the benefits of dialogic curriculum in meeting the objectives of the Common Core State Standards, this book with its companion website is an ideal resource for teacher development.

**Mary M. Juzwik** is associate professor of language and literacy in the Department of Teacher Education at Michigan State University (MSU), and co-editor of the journal *Research in the Teaching of English*. **Carlin Borsheim-Black** is assistant professor of English language and literature at Central Michigan University (CMU). **Samantha Caughlan** is an assistant professor of English education in the Department of Teacher Education at MSU. **Anne Heintz** is an adjunct professor in the Master of Arts in Educational Technology program at MSU.

## Teachers College Press
**TEACHERS COLLEGE** | COLUMBIA UNIVERSITY
WWW.TCPRESS.COM

ISBN 978-0-8077-5467-2

90000>

9 780807 754672